Make That Call!

To Tracey, Michael, Sophie and Adam

THE SUNDAY TIMES

Make That Call!

SECOND EDITION

Iain Maitland

KOGAN PAGE | CREATING SUCCESS

First South Asian Edition 2000

Kogan Page India Private Limited
4325/3 Ansari Road
New Delhi 110 002.

This edition is for sale in India, Bangladesh, Nepal, Pakistan and Sri Lanka only. Not for export elsewhere.

ISBN 81-7554-131-8

Published by Vinod Vasishtha for Kogan Page India Private Limited, 4325/3 Ansari Road, Daryaganj, New Delhi 110 002, and printed at Rajkamal Electric Press, Delhi 110 033.

contents

introduction 1

1. **making difficult calls** 2
planning calls 2; handling conversations 4; follow-up calls 7; winning tactics: your step-by-step checklist 8

2. **speaking to customers** 11
the enquiry about products or services 12; calling a prospective customer 13; asking for an introduction to a would-be customer 15; making a sales presentation 17; the request for a discount, positive response 19; the request for a discount, negative response 20; the request for credit, positive response 21; the request for credit, negative response 23; closing a sale 24; getting through a personal assistant 26; following up a sale 27; the request for a customer reference 29; apologising for undelivered goods 30; the complaint about products or services 32; answering a complaint, positive response 34; answering a complaint, negative response 35; chasing a debt, first call 37; chasing a debt, second call 39; chasing a debt, third call 40; the request for a delayed payment schedule, positive response 42; the request for a delayed payment proposal, negative response 44; calling a customer who has not used their account for some time 45; calling a customer who has closed their account 47

3. **talking to suppliers** 50
the call from a sales representative 51; the call from a market researcher 52; the call from a persistent sales representative 54; stopping unwanted sales calls 55; enquiring about goods and services 56; requesting a discount 57; asking for credit terms 59; chasing overdue products or services, agreeable delivery date 60; chasing overdue products or services, disagreeable delivery date 62; rejecting damaged goods 63; making a complaint, accepted 65; making a complaint, rejected 66; querying a bill 68; asking to return unsold goods 69; requesting increased credit facilities 70; the demand for payment 71; asking for extended credit facilities, accepted 72; asking for extended credit facilities, refused 74

4. **conversing with employees** 76
the speculative enquiry about a possible job opportunity 77; inviting a job applicant to an interview 78; conducting a telephone interview 80; the enquiry from a job applicant 82; asking for a reference 83; making a job offer, accepted 85; making a job offer, rejected 87; the enquiry from a job applicant 89; the notification of sickness 90; calling an absent employee 92; counselling an unhappy employee with work-related problems 94; counselling an unhappy employee with personal difficulties 96; thanking a colleague 97; praising an employee 98; encouraging an employee to improve 99; disciplining an employee 102; giving a reference about an employee 104

5. **handling personal calls** 107
enquiring about prospective job opportunities, known contact 107; enquiring about prospective job opportunities, unknown contact 109; the invitation to an interview 110; the telephone interview 112; the offer of employment, positive response 114; the offer of employment, negative response 117; asking for a meeting 118; the request for a meeting, positive response 119; the request for a meeting, negative response 121; introducing an associate to a third

party 122; thanking an associate for an introduction 123; congratulating someone on their promotion 125; congratulating someone on an award 126; thanking someone for an award 127; thanking someone for a present 128; sympathising with someone on the loss of their job 129; sympathising with someone on a business failure 131; sympathising with someone on the death of their partner 133

6. **managing miscellaneous calls** **136**
asking for a donation 136; thanking someone for a donation 138; the request for a donation, positive response 140; the request for a donation, negative response 141; asking for a favour 142; the request for a favour, positive response 143; the request for a favour, negative response 144; offering a favour 145; the offer of a favour, positive response 146; the offer of a favour, negative response 147; calling a newsdesk 148; calling a features editor 150; the press interview 151; the radio interview 152; declining an interview 154; correcting an inaccurate story 156; congratulating someone on a favourable story 157; reminding someone of a promise 158; reminding someone of an obligation 160; inviting someone to an event 161; the invitation to an event, positive response 163; the invitation to an event, negative response 164; calling the emergency services 165; the obscene telephone call 166; the silent telephone call 167

introduction

Make That Call! enables you to handle the trickiest telephone calls, whatever their nature. It is ideal if you have to make or receive difficult phone calls as part of your job, and are unsure what to say and how to say it. With the help of 101 sample conversations and explanatory comments, this book tells you all you need to know.

Chapter 1 provides a step-by-step guide to making or receiving tricky telephone calls, so that you can plan, handle and follow up on any call successfully.

Chapters 2–6 look at the hardest phone calls you may have to manage, including:

- chasing customers for outstanding payments;
- negotiating discounts from suppliers;
- disciplining employees;
- and even dealing with silent phone calls!

The most effective way to make or receive a difficult call is to check the contents list on pages v–vii, see which type of call is the most relevant, and read the conversation and its explanatory comments. For the fullest understanding of handling tricky phone calls, you can work through the book in the normal way. Whatever you choose, you'll learning the winning tactics for successful telephone calls.

Iain Maitland

1

making difficult calls

Difficult telephone calls can be grouped into two categories: outgoing ones as diverse as chasing a debt and reminding someone of an unkept promise, and incoming ones as varied as a complaint about products or services and a press or radio interview. Whatever type of call is being made or received, you need to plan properly, to handle the conversation effectively, and to follow it through afterwards, doing whatever needs to be done to consolidate that successful call.

planning calls

Whether you are making or receiving calls, the key to managing them well is preparation. You do not necessarily need to plan extensively or in great detail, but it is useful to know something about *who* you are talking to, *when* you are going to speak to them and from *where*, *what* you will say and *how* you will persuade them to do what you want. Much of this can be worked out in your head and, after a while, it will become second nature to you.

who?

Consider who you will be speaking to, how well you know them and what they are like, as far as this is possible. This will affect how you address them – in a friendly manner to 'Sue' who is a former colleague, or more formally to 'Mr Houseman' who is a prospective employer. Your assessment (which need not take long to do) will also enable you to decide on their levels of knowledge and understanding of the situation and how to talk to them. You may have to provide simple explanations for a layperson, for example, whereas a specialist would be more familiar with technical details.

when?

Think carefully about the best time to telephone people. This is usually when it is most likely to be convenient and agreeable for them. Typically, before 10 am may be unsuitable because they are arriving at work, opening their post, and so on. Between 12 and 2 o'clock may coincide with their lunchbreak. After 5.00, they may be tidying up and going home. Incoming calls may occur at any time, so be ready for them, whatever the hour. Make sure that you have enough time to deal with them properly. If not, have an answering machine switched on and then return calls at the earliest opportunity.

where?

Whether it is an outgoing or an incoming call, it is sensible to talk in a quiet room. This may seem to be an obvious point, but it is one that many people ignore to their cost when they may be disturbed by noise from an adjoining office or be interrupted by a colleague. Again, if you are unable to have a telephone conversation in a quiet office, switch on your answering machine and return the call at a more suitable time. Wherever you hold a telephone conversation, make sure that you have a pen or pencil and notepaper to hand so that you can make notes. And have a spare pen or pencil available, just in case you need it.

what?

When you speak to someone on the phone, you should have a good idea of what you want to discuss with them. Make a checklist of the main points so that you can refer to them – for example, the person's name, their extension number, the questions you want to raise and the comments you wish to make. If you are trying to sell a product, you might list its benefits, for easy reference. Use these as reminders, though, not as a script, which is too restricting and will make you sound stilted. Have any supporting documentation close by you as well – for example, invoices, curricula vitae, previous correspondence, and so on.

how?

Contemplate how you will persuade the person you are talking to, to do what you want. Achieve this by telling them what *they* want to know, not what *you* want to say. For example, explain how the new product you are selling will benefit them if they buy it, rather than what you like about it. Also, make it easy for them to respond in the required manner – for example, fax through details of the product and an order form immediately after the conversation.

handling conversations

Whether you are making outgoing calls or receiving incoming ones, you should be ready and able to handle conversations effectively, whatever the type of call. Whoever you are talking to and whatever you have to say, many conversations will proceed along similar lines, so you should be ready to *start* one properly, to *speak* and to *listen*, to *ask* and *answer* questions, and to *finish* the conversation in a polite and businesslike way.

starting

When you call someone, you should know not only their name but its correct pronunciation, their extension number if it is appropriate, what you are telephoning about and want. When said in a bright and positive way, this will give you your opening comments: 'Hello. Please will you put me through to Juanita di Carlos on extension 401. Thank you. Ms di Carlos? Hello, my name is John Greene. I'm telephoning about ...'

With incoming calls, you must sound prepared and professional in your manner. '213242, David Adams speaking' is usually sufficient if you are answering the phone in person. 'Hello, this is Sean Wicks. Please leave your name, number and a brief message after the tone. I'll get back to you by the end of the day' may be an appropriate message on an answering machine. It is important to keep such a message short and businesslike, avoiding anything humorous or outlandish, which can be offputting.

speaking

Because it is essential that you are heard clearly, it may be unwise to make difficult phone calls from a mobile telephone, which can be temperamental at times. Make sure that you are understood, which may mean using simple and unambiguous language rather than slang, jargon and technical expressions. Spell out names and difficult words and repeat numbers, as required. It can be a good idea to tape your voice and play it back to check that you speak steadily and do not roll, slur or mumble your words. Make certain that you speak into the mouthpiece, too.

listening

Obvious though it may seem, you must listen carefully to what the other person is saying. It is all too easy to make the mistake of mulling over what you have just said (or should have said) or what you want to say next. Consequently, you run the risk of mishearing and making a nonsensical reply, or even speaking over the top of their comments, which may cause offence. It is courteous to be heard to be listening by saying 'mmm', 'yes' and 'go on...' during pauses, and by asking them to spell difficult names, especially when you want to note something down.

questioning

Make a note in your checklist of any questions you wish to ask during the conversation. 'Open' questions beginning with 'What?', 'How?' and 'Why?' will encourage the other person to talk, to explain and to give their thoughts and opinions. 'Closed' questions such as 'Can you offer a 10 per cent discount?' and 'Have you paid your bill?' should bring a vague and rambling statement to an end and produce a short, direct answer.

answering

Keep your answers to any questions raised as brief and as pertinent as possible. You will find it helpful when answering questions to refer to the notes you jotted down before you began the conversation and the relevant documents that are close at hand. If you have received an unexpected call, it is always advisable to take the person's details and return the call shortly afterwards when you have all the facts available, rather than try to manage a conversation without being prepared for it.

finishing

Generally, you should finish a conversation by outlining what has been discussed, encouraging the other person to agree with it and making it as easy as possible for them to do so, if appropriate. Tell them what will happen next and end on an amicable note – for example, 'So, we're agreed on a 10 per cent discount then, Stephen... Good... I'll get the brochure and order form off to you tonight by first-class post, and ask Lorraine to call on you on Friday to finalise everything. Nice to speak to you again, Stephen... We'll talk again soon.'

follow-up calls

Relatively few calls are made or received in isolation; the vast majority require some form of follow-up action. This can vary from *making notes* to *sending a letter* confirming the main points of what was discussed, to implementing whatever you have agreed. You may even have to make or receive further calls in due course, depending on the circumstances.

notes

It is a good idea to jot down notes as and when appropriate during a conversation, and to record these more formally immediately afterwards while the key points remain fresh in your memory. For example, if you called a customer to try to make a sale or contacted a job applicant to invite them to a selection interview, you might note the date and time of the call, the name and details of the recipient, what was discussed and agreed, and what will happen next. Such notes act as an aide-mémoire for you and any colleagues who are involved, and (often as important) as a source of reference in case of disputes.

other activities

In some situations, it may be advisable to follow your conversation with a letter summarising what was discussed and agreed by both sides – perhaps when you have complained about goods or services, rejected delivery of damaged items or made an offer of employment to a successful job candidate. This is essential if it involves (potential) disagreements and possible legal action.

You should then implement whatever you have agreed to do as soon as possible – for example, forwarding sales literature and order forms, despatching or collecting goods, arranging for a sales representative to visit, and so on. If you have made a note to make a further phone call, perhaps when you are chasing up an overdue invoice or account, you should do this at the stated time.

winning tactics: your step-by-step checklist

1. The key to a successful telephone call is preparation. Consider who you will be talking to, when and from where, as well as what you will say, and how you will say it.
2. Discover as much as you can about the person you will be speaking with. In particular, this will help you to assess their understanding of a subject and how you should talk to them about it.
3. Outgoing calls should be made usually when it is most convenient for the other person to receive them. Incoming calls should be received only when you have sufficient time to handle them. If not, use an answering machine and return calls when it is more convenient.

4. All telephone conversations should be dealt with in a quiet and undisturbed room. Again, use an answering machine as and when necessary, returning calls when it is more peaceful. Have a pen and paper at hand to make notes.
5. Know what you are going to say in a conversation. Have a checklist of points that need to be raised close by for reference purposes. Similarly, have any supporting documentation readily available, too.
6. Tell the other person what they want to know, not what you want to tell them. Typically, they will want to know how they will benefit from the conversation. Make it easy for them to respond in the way that you want them to – for example, be ready to take an order over the phone.
7. Know how to start a call properly. You should be able to speak and to listen. Be prepared to ask and answer questions. Know how to end a conversation in a polite and businesslike manner.
8. Begin all conversations in a bright and professional way. Do not have unorthodox messages on answering machines, as these can sound unprofessional.
9. Make sure that you can be heard clearly. Tape yourself and play back the recording to identify areas for improvement. Ensure that you are understood by using plain, straightforward words and expressions.
10. Listen closely to what is being said to you. Make it obvious that you are listening by making encouraging noises, as and when relevant.
11. Make a note of any questions you wish to ask. Open questions should produce detailed, explanatory answers. Closed questions should force direct answers from the other person.
12. Provide short, concise answers to questions. Refer to supporting documentation, when necessary. Return

calls if the information needed is not immediately to hand.

13. Try to finish in agreement with the other person. Indicate what will happen next, if appropriate.
14. Always follow up a conversation with any action that may be required to complete it successfully. This will often involve making notes or carrying out other activities.
15. Make notes during the call if this can be done without disrupting the flow of the conversation. If not, do it immediately afterwards, when everything is still fresh in your mind.
16. Similarly, send a letter, sales catalogues, price lists, or do whatever is required, as soon as possible after the conversation.
17. Congratulate yourself – you've made a winning business call!

2

speaking to customers

Quite simply, customers are a firm's most important asset – without them, it cannot exist. To survive, prosper and expand, a business must either keep acquiring new customers or increase its trade with its existing customer base. Speaking to prospective and present customers on the telephone can help a business to achieve these aims. Most customer-related calls can be divided into three categories:

- those that persuade would-be and current customers to buy goods and services from you;
- those that deal with customer complaints, and, hopefully, resolve them in a prompt and agreeable manner;
- those that chase up outstanding money and customers who have not purchased anything from you for some time.

the enquiry about products or services

'260. Andrew King speaking. How can I help you?'

'You've got a special offer on at the moment on your baby clothes. Can you tell me about it?'

'Yes. We're currently offering 25 per cent off our summer range on orders of £500 or more received by the end of the month. The offer applies to all leading names – Babytime, Kidzkits, Hammertons and ZZZ-Wear. Stocks are limited and are being sold on a first-come, first-served basis. I can take an order over the phone, if you'd like me to.'

'Er, I'll think about it. When did you say the offer ends?'

'Next Friday, the last day of the month. If you give me your name and contact details, I'll drop an order form in the post to you tonight.'

'Okay, yes. It's Babyland in Woodridge, Sussex. I've an account with you. My name's Kay Banks. I'm the owner.'

'Thank you, Miss Banks. I'll send you a form tonight so that you can place an order in time for next Friday. And don't forget, you can always order over the phone if you prefer. My name's Andrew King and I'm on extension 260. I'm always here to help...'

comments

1. Handling an incoming enquiry about your goods or services seems easy – and it is, but only if it is approached correctly. Unfortunately, many people try too hard to make an immediate sale and, as a consequence, drive a prospective customer away. It is far better simply to follow their lead, to give them the

information they seek and, if possible, to obtain some details about them so that you can follow up this call later if an order is not received shortly afterwards. If you are too insistent at the outset, they will exercise the ultimate rebuff, and put down the phone.

2. Answer the phone as specified by your company – that is, promptly and giving clearly your extension number and name followed by a greeting such as 'How can I help you?' Have the information they request readily available (or, if not, return their call as soon as you have obtained it). Provide brief details in response to their questions, mentioning the benefits for them, but without labouring the points. Encourage them to place an order now or soon by referring to any special offers, time limits, and the like. Conclude by offering to send further details or arranging for a representative to call. At the very least, obtain their name and phone number so that you can follow up the call, as necessary. Always set up that follow-through opportunity.

calling a prospective customer

'Hello, Mr Berbeck. My name's Lillie Stevens from Brownings Office Supplies in Brigtown. I've been given your number by Shirley Thomsett at EBC Communications. I understand we have something in common.'

'Have we? What's that, then?'

'Well, Brownings provide office equipment and stationery to several firms in your area, including Willards, Browne–Wilkins and Tubbs. We don't supply you and I'd like to take just two minutes to tell you what we can offer...'

'All right, you've got two minutes, starting now.'

'Okay. We've been established for more than 12 years. We carry in stock the widest range of word processors, printers, photocopiers and fax machines, and at very competitive prices. We supply office stationery, too – everything you can think of – and offer next-day delivery on all orders. What exactly are you looking for, Mr Berbeck?'

'You say you supply all sorts of office stationery. Tell me, do you carry...?'

comments

1. 'Cold-calling' an unknown customer is always difficult. You must accept before you begin that most people will not want to talk to you, and a number of these will tell you so, often quite forcefully. Numerous calls (as many as 20) will have to be made in order to find one that goes beyond your introduction and develops into a conversation.
2. Begin by introducing yourself briefly and politely, and mentioning any people whom you both know, if appropriate. Explain why you are calling and establish your credibility by referring to any mutually known customers that you have, if this is relevant. Indicate that you will take up no more than a couple of minutes of their time and that it will prove to be worthwhile to them. Don't rush and garble this introduction because you expect rejection – such an approach only increases the chances of this happening.
3. Then talk in broad, positive terms about your firm, its goods and services, as relevant to this particular customer. Don't be too specific about prices or whatever at this stage, as this will answer their questions, often before they have even thought of them. Make them curious and eager to learn more. When they ask that first question, you know you've got them hooked, as seen in the example.

4. Find out what you can about the customer and their requirements with regard to whatever you are selling. Keep them talking and interested. Most people enjoy talking about themselves. As and when appropriate, indicate how they would benefit from having your product or using your service. Have a list of benefits to hand that you can refer to, as necessary.
5. Your prospects of making a sale from this initial canvassing call are remote, not least because most people need time to think things over before they make a decision to buy, especially if it will be a major purchase. Thus, you should view this call as preparatory work for later ones, as shown on pages 24 and 27. Arrange to send further information to them and agree a date when you can call back to discuss the matter further, or even to pay them a visit. Conclude by thanking them for their time and/or for talking to you.

asking for an introduction to a would-be customer

'I wonder if you can do me a favour, Nick? Would you introduce me to Margaret Lewis at Bronsons? I've heard she's looking for some computer support services and as we've just diversified into that area, we might be able to come to some arrangement.'

'Yeah, sure. What do you want me to say?'

'Well, as you know, we've been in business here for eight years, offer support services on all leading computers and provide a same-day service and loan equipment as and when appropriate.'

'Okay, got it. Sounds good.'

'Could you call her for me either today or tomorrow? I'll then get in touch on Thursday or Friday to see if I can set up a meeting.'

'No problem. I'm due to ring her anyway on another matter, so it's no trouble at all.'

'Thanks very much indeed, Nick. I appreciate your help. Thank you.'

comments

1. Often, an introduction made by an intermediary provides you with the best prospect of making a sale and, hopefully, going on to establish a long-term trading relationship with a customer. To make a success of this call, you need to know the go-between well enough to ask such a favour, and they must have sufficient confidence in you to make what amounts to a recommendation. Also, they have to be willing to act as an intermediary, and they must know the prospective customer equally well and be thought of highly by them!
2. If, and only if, all these criteria are fulfilled, this call becomes relatively easy. Various points need to be made in sequence. Request the introduction and say why it might benefit the prospective customer and you. Give the go-between some brief details about you to pass on, if their memory needs to be refreshed or nudged in the right direction. Say what you want them to do and by when. Outline what you will then do afterwards. Avoid stating what is in it for them since this sounds like a clumsy bribe. A 'thank you' is sufficient.

making a sales presentation

'Gerry?... It's Maureen Wagstaffe at Bakers. We spoke last week about the problems you've had with stock deliveries and agreed to talk again today. Have you received our catalogue?'

'Yes, I've had a look through it.'

'That's great. I just wanted to spend a couple of minutes on it with you.'

'Go on, then. Tell me what you can do to solve our problems.'

'Well, we can supply everything you're currently getting from three or four other sources, which will make ordering easier for you. We despatch within 48 hours of receiving your order for next-day delivery, so you'll know what you're getting and when. And by my calculations, we're 10 per cent cheaper than your other suppliers, too, so you'll save money as well.'

'That sounds promising, but I'll tell you what worries me. Who does your deliveries? We have a lot of problems with damaged items being delivered to us. How can we be sure that won't happen with you?'

'I know how you feel, Gerry. That's incredibly frustrating, both for you and for us. That's why we've used our own drivers and lorries for the past year and haven't had any difficulties yet. I'm sure Janet David at SPS and Mary Worth at Heckles will confirm that. If anything did happen, we would get a replacement off to you straight away, that same day.'

'That sounds good to me. Okay, where do we go from here?'

comments

1. You should be able to follow up your original canvassing call to a prospective customer or an introduction via an intermediary (see pages 13 and 15 respectively) with a more detailed call presenting your products or services for sale. As with all calls, it is important that you are well prepared, but especially so in this situation, not least by having the facts and figures about the product (or whatever) to hand, along with a list of its key benefits for this customer.
2. Reintroduce yourself, state that you are telephoning as agreed, and check that any information sent has been received. Say that you would like to go over what was discussed previously, emphasising your intention to do this swiftly. Then do it.
3. Ask further questions as and when appropriate to ascertain the customer's exact wants and needs as closely as you can. Then match the benefits that are offered by your goods or services with these specific wants and needs, explaining briefly how they will be satisfied by them. Concentrate exclusively on these matching benefits, rather than on other (interesting but) irrelevant ones.
4. Be ready to handle any queries or objections. Typically, these are about the price, the reliability of a product, and/or your ability to deliver a quality service, as and when agreed. This is where your preparations and those facts, figures and notes will prove invaluable to you. For example, you might refer to discounts that can be offered, or other well-known customers who can vouch for you.
5. Sometimes, the recipient of your call will be willing to place an order or to buy goods by credit card over the phone; if so, you should take the necessary details, follow this with written confirmation, and then

process the transaction as promptly as possible. However, it is more likely that they will want to take time to think about it, or perhaps they will decline your offer immediately. If this happens, you can probe gently to uncover their concerns and try to resolve them. Alternatively, you can arrange to speak again at a later date.

the request for a discount, positive response

'So what sort of discount can you offer me?'

'5 per cent for payment in advance, cash on collection or cash on delivery. 5 per cent for orders over £1,000.'

'I'm looking for 10 per cent. I'll pay cash on collection and will order £500 now, with more regular orders later on if the first lot sells well.'

'Well, we can offer a first-time buyer's discount, too, so yes, we can give you 10 per cent on this occasion. Our normal trading terms will apply after that. They are very competitive in comparison to other firms...'

comments

1. From time to time, you will be asked for a discount in excess of what you usually offer and will then need to decide whether to accept or reject this request. Often, you will feel inclined to provide an improved prompt-payment discount to speed up your cash-flow, or a better bulk-buy discount to avoid losing a substantial sale to a rival, or a first-time buyer's discount to initiate a trading relationship. Be careful, though,

accepting only if it is fair to your other customers and will not set an unviable precedent. Customers have a habit of discovering the discounts that others are receiving and will want the same, both now and in the future.

2. During this conversation, it is wise to specify your normal trading terms and conditions, why you are willing to exceed them on this occasion, and what trading terms and conditions will apply in the future. Obviously, if a positive response seems unfair on your remaining customers and/or would establish an unfavourable precedent, then it may be more sensible to respond in a negative manner, as below.

the request for a discount, negative response

'... My total order will be about £300. Can you give me 20 per cent off the list price for that?'

'Unfortunately not. We need to keep to our list prices. However, I'm sure we can offer you a great deal.'

'Such as?'

'We can offer various early settlement and bulk purchase discounts. Would you be paying cash?'

'If the price is right.'

'And how many units would you be buying?'

'Eight or nine.'

'Well, on that basis, how about...?'

comments

1. Often, you will not feel able to respond positively to a prospective customer's request for a discount, because they ask for more than you would normally offer, or acceptance would be unfair on your other customers, or it would simply be unprofitable for you. Sometimes, it will be because they want a discount on an extremely small order – an increasingly common request nowadays.
2. Begin by rejecting the request, politely but firmly. Give a reason, which should be broad and diplomatic – 'we can only offer what other customers are given…', as an example.
3. Set out what you can offer and negotiate accordingly. Obviously, you will be seeking a compromise deal that suits both parties, allows you to make a profit on this and future transactions, and does not create difficulties for you with your other customers.
4. As an alternative to negotiating over the telephone, it may be a good idea to persuade them to agree to a sales agent calling on them. This would then enable you to show and demonstrate the relevant goods and increase your chances of negotiating to a successful conclusion.

the request for credit, positive response

'… So, can you offer us a credit account, Mr Wiseman?'

'I'm sure we can come to some arrangement, Miss Hopkins. We ask for one bank and two trade references before opening credit accounts. Can you let us have details of suggested referees with your first order?'

'Yes, no problem.'

'If you're happy for me to phone your trade referees, that'll speed up the order considerably.'

'Yes, I'm happy for you to do that.'

'Okay, well assuming all is well – and I'm sure it will be – we can offer you a £1,000 credit limit, with invoices due for payment within 30 days of issue. We do put an automatic stop on all overdue accounts, although I'm sure that won't affect you.'

'That sounds fine to me. It's what I was looking for.'

'Obviously, if you'd prefer to pay on a cash-with-order or cash-on-delivery basis, we can also give you a 5 per cent discount...'

comments

1. Most customers want to trade on credit terms and will request this facility before or at an early stage of their dealings with you. Ideally, of course, you would deal with cash in advance or at least not provide credit until customers have shown themselves to be reliable and trustworthy in their transactions with your firm. However, you may feel obliged to accept the request straight away – not least, perhaps, because you would rather have delayed incomings from this source than risk receiving nothing at all.
2. In the course of such a conversation, you must obtain details of referees whom you can approach for reference purposes – their bankers (whom you will need to contact in writing through your own bank) and two trade suppliers who can be telephoned (with permission) for informal, off-the-record comments. Informal discussions are always more revealing than comments put in writing.

3. Also, set some restraints on this credit facility, specifying a credit limit, payment terms and conditions, and, briefly, the importance of adhering to these and the possible consequences of not doing so. Phrase these comments diplomatically!
4. Take the opportunity to stress the benefits of the alternatives to using credit facilities, focusing on cash-with-order, cash-on-collection/delivery and prompt payment discounts, in particular. This is especially significant if a healthy cash-flow is as important to your concern as it is to the majority of businesses. Encourage customers to help themselves and you!
5. Evidently, new customers' accounts should be monitored closely in the early days, with any signs of delay being tackled swiftly and firmly. Refer to pages 37, 39 and 40 for examples of calls chasing overdue bills.

the request for credit, negative response

'... No, unfortunately, we're not opening new credit accounts at the present time because of trading conditions. But we'd be very happy to look at this again in, say, six months.'

'I see. That's rather disappointing, Mr Grant.'

'However, we can offer you 6 per cent off all orders paid for on a cash-with-order or cash-on-collection basis, and we are currently despatching within 24 hours of receipt of orders. If you come in, you can also look at our full range of merchandise, including...'

comments

1. There will be occasions when you will feel that you have to refuse a request for a credit account. This is usually because it is a new business with no track record and cannot provide references, or it is an established firm that offers poor references, or has a mixed credit history with you.
2. Try to make a clear and unmistakable refusal at the beginning of the conversation so that it does not drift on endlessly. Give your reason – for example, this may need to be diplomatic rather than ruthlessly honest, especially if you want to retain their custom. To achieve this, it is a good idea to be hopeful and encouraging about the future, typically suggesting a review at a later date. (Even if the answer will still be 'no', it can persuade them to keep trading and to improve their dealings.) Also, you can indicate the benefits of the existing arrangement, sounding cheerful and upbeat throughout.
3. Obviously, if you think that such a refusal may result in the customer taking their business elsewhere, you will have to weigh this possibility alongside the benefits of retaining their custom by providing credit facilities; you will also have to consider that you may receive delayed or late payments from them, or even none at all. Clearly, this is a difficult choice, so think carefully.

closing a sale

'... Now, we can do all that for you, Janet, no problem at all. The only thing is – and it's only fair to tell you this – we only had a few of these left in stock when I checked this morning, and they're being sold on a "first-come, first-served" basis. Would you like me to get one off to you today, before they've all gone?'

comments

1. This is a tricky call to make, especially if the prospective customer originally contacted you but has not advanced this initial enquiry, or you cold-called them, followed this with a sales presentation but did not take an order or make a sale afterwards (see pages 12, 13 and 17 respectively). You need to press hard enough to win them over, but not so much that you alienate them completely.
2. Make your first comments bright and cheerful, introducing yourself again, referring to previous communications between you and asking if they would like further information about whatever interested them. Be positive and upbeat, and not at all reproachful or apologetic. Be prepared for them to rebuff you at this stage and back off gracefully if this occurs, rather than pressing on, as this will inevitably lead to an argument, and ill feeling.
3. If they remain interested but genuinely undecided, tell them about the product, service or whatever again, stressing the benefits and what is in it for them if they bought or used it. Welcome any queries or objections they may have, probe gently to uncover their full extent, test them with one or two further questions to check that these are genuine, and then answer them. Match the benefits of the product or service with the needs of this prospective customer as and when possible.
4. To encourage them to place an order, it can be a good idea to worry them a little, as seen in the example, by

indicating that stocks are limited, and that prices are due to rise shortly, or whatever. Give them the chance to order by taking their credit card details, by offering to take cash-on-delivery, or by sending a sales representative to take the order, and then close the sale.

getting through a personal assistant

'Morning, can you put me through to Doug, please?'

'Who's calling, please?'

'It's Tom here, from Bendex.'

'Can I ask what it's about?'

'Yes, I need to talk to him about our new summer range of goods.'

'Hold on... No, I'm sorry, he's busy at the moment.'

'When will he be free?'

'He is extremely busy at the moment. Can I help you at all?'

'I really do need to speak to Doug. It will only take a couple of minutes, and I'm sure he'd be interested. What time does he finish work? Perhaps I could give him a quick call then.'

'Well, you could try him after five o'clock...'

comments

1. There may be occasions when you will not automatically get through to a potential customer and will speak instead to a personal assistant whose job includes stopping troublesome and/or time-consuming

calls from reaching their employer. There are various dos and don'ts to follow in this situation that should help you to make contact with the person you really want to talk to.

2. Sound confident and self-assured as you start to speak, intimating that you know the prospective customer well and are expecting a warm welcome. This can often result in your being put through straight away – the personal assistant may assume that you are a close friend or a well-established business contact.
3. Don't give out any information about the reason for your call unless you are pressed, and even then, you should make it clear that the call is an important one for that person and only they can deal with the matter; otherwise, the personal assistant may try to handle it, especially if they do not consider it to be important.
4. If you are put through, you can canvass the person's views, make a sales presentation or attempt to close a sale, as appropriate (see pages 17 and 24). Should the personal assistant say that the person is busy, thank them and ask when that person will be free to talk to you. Call back at the suggested time. If you are told that they are 'always busy' (a polite way of saying 'don't call back') stress that you will be very brief and will take up only a few minutes of their time. If this still fails, it may be more appropriate to send a fax, letter, or to approach someone else in the company.

following up a sale

'Hello, Miss Dwyer. It's April Workington at Denton & Co. I'm just ringing to thank you for your order 23 and to see when you received it.'

'Oh, hi. Yes, we received it a couple of days back. It came very quickly.'

'Excellent. As I said when we last spoke, we do operate a same day despatch service for our "standard" items, which does enable you to order goods only as and when you need them, and you can be assured of a prompt delivery. I'm sure this will help you with your stock planning and control in the future.'

'Yes. I think it'll be useful to us.'

'Which goods sell most quickly in your business, Miss Dwyer?'

comments

1. It is often worthwhile to make a follow-up call to a customer after a sale, especially if it is a first-time and/or large purchase. This call serves several purposes. It can help to cement a newly established relationship by showing that you care. Also, it enables you to identify the positive and negative aspects of the transaction and to remedy any shortcomings as quickly as possible. It helps to pave the way for future orders too, perhaps even immediately on occasions.
2. Begin by thanking them for their order and checking that they have received it (leaving sufficient time between the despatch of the goods and your call to ensure that they will have done). Be careful not to ask if everything is all right (or something similar) as this will create doubt and the rather alarming suspicion that you expected problems to arise. Clearly, this is not reassuring.
3. Your next comments should develop from the customer's response and their subsequent statements. If favourable, you should take the opportunity to promote your firm's strengths and how these can be of benefit to that customer on a long-term basis, as shown in the example conversation. If they are dissat-

isfied, you should try to resolve their complaint immediately, as illustrated on page 34.

4. If appropriate, seek to obtain a further order by identifying their present wants and needs, matching the benefits of trading with your firm with these requirements, and making it easy for them to place an immediate order. Typically, you might offer to fill out an order form for them over the telephone, and fax through a copy of it for their records.

the request for a customer reference

'What can you tell me about Laflin and Co, then?'

'They've been trading with us for 18 months now. For the first six months, they had a cash account, paying cash on collection of their goods. For the past year, they've had a credit account with a £2,000 limit that they have kept within, and bills have been paid in 30 days.'

'So what you're saying is that they're reliable and trustworthy, and good for credit facilities with us.'

'As I say, they've been customers of ours for 18 months. To date, they have kept to their credit limit and settled their bills at the agreed time...'

comments

1. Giving a reference about a customer is rarely as easy as it seems, especially over the telephone when you may be expected to talk at length and revealingly about them. If you give too favourable a reference, the person requesting the reference may be unhappy with

you if that customer does not subsequently fulfil expectations. If you are unfavourable about them, the customer might learn of it and stop trading with you as a consequence. Be careful!

2. By far the best approach in the circumstances is to concentrate on providing the facts, which cannot be disputed. It is sensible to make these fairly generalised, unless you have been authorised by the customer to give specific facts and figures. Even though a conversation of this nature tends to have a rather informal, off-the-record feel to it (especially if you know the caller well), it is advisable to avoid providing personal opinions, recommendations or criticisms. Give only the facts and let the other person reach their own conclusions.

apologising for undelivered goods

'... Hello, this is Matt Draper at Buzzbox. I'm phoning with regard to your order number 52, dated 7 July, for 60 AZ-42s. There's been a delay because of import problems and I wanted to apologise to you for this.'

'Oh, right... When will we get it, then?'

'We were telephoned this morning to say they were sent yesterday, so we expect to receive them by the middle of next week, and they'll then be with you by Monday or Tuesday of the following week – the 9th or 10th.'

'No, no, that's a bit too late for us... um... '

'I'll tell you what I can do. We've some of the AZ-40s in stock. I can send you 60 of those today by Express Delivery. They'll be with you in the morning.'

'That's an idea. What's the difference in price though?'

'The '40s are another pound each, but we'll do them at the same price as the '42s on this occasion... '

comments

1. The vast majority of those businesses that are faced with not being able to deliver an order on time simply do nothing and hope that they can subsequently forward the goods when they are available. Not surprisingly, these firms run the risk of causing offence, damaging relations with their customers and losing them to their more conscientious rivals. As often as not, this prospect can be avoided, and relations even improved, simply by making an explanatory phone call as soon as a problem becomes apparent.
2. Start the conversation by referring to the order – its number, date and contents, as appropriate. Then give briefly a reason for the delay and apologise for it. Do not dwell on the reason – the customer is not that interested and just wants to know how it affects them. State when the order will be delivered, providing a specific rather than a generalised date if possible, but only if you are able to adhere to it.
3. If they agree with this, you can draw the call to a close, thanking them and apologising again before you say goodbye. If they express doubt and it looks as though you may lose the order, you should be ready to offer an alternative – ideally, similar goods at the same (or lower) prices that can be despatched straight away. If necessary, offer a discount off the usual prices of these goods because of the inconvenience caused by the delay.

the complaint about products or services

'Babes of Ipstone. Helen speaking. How can I help you?'

'Hello. I'm ringing about a pram you sold me that is now falling apart. I want to know how I can get my money back.'

'I see. Well, I'm sorry to hear you're unhappy. Let me take some details. Can you tell me your name and when you bought the pram, please?'

'Yes, it's Mrs Williamson, 3 Thornes Way on the Faulkeners Road estate. I bought it in January.'

'Thank you. Can you tell me what make of pram it is, Mrs Williamson, and why you are unhappy with it?'

'Yes, it's a red one with a diamond-shaped interior. I'm unhappy because it's falling apart. It's rubbish.'

'Red with a diamond-patterned interior... that sounds like a Hammex "Ranger". Can you tell me a bit more about why you're unhappy exactly?'

'Well, the cover round my baby's legs is all loose and the bottom bit – the chassis thing – leans to one side. I've never seen anything like it. It's dreadful. My husband says we should go down to the trading standards people, but I said I'd ring you first to see if you'll give us our money back.'

'I see. Well, if we can get it into the workshop and have a look at it, we'll be able to come back to you by the end of the day and can then take it from there. Are you in the town today?'

comments

1. Telephone complaints are always tricky to handle. Often, they are unexpected, you are unfamiliar with the facts and the customer is angry, perhaps to the point of being incoherent. In such circumstances, it may be best not to try to resolve the complaint straight away.
2. In order to decide whether to accept or reject the complaint, you need to concentrate on getting the who–what–when–where–why–how? facts of the matter from the caller. As in the example, ask questions to obtain this information from them.
3. Until you have investigated the matter fully and discovered the other side of the story (if there is one), you will not know if this is a genuine complaint or perhaps an attempt to take advantage of your good nature. In the example, the customer may be trying to swap her pram for a new pushchair! Hence, you should be polite and sympathetic to their feelings throughout the conversation, but without admitting faults or committing yourself to any requested course of action, such as making a refund. Indicate that you will look into the situation and come back to them at a particular time, making sure that you can do so, to avoid generating unnecessary ill feeling and unpleasantness.
4. If, on investigation, you believe that it is a valid complaint, you can give a positive response to remedy the situation, as below. Alternatively, you will respond in a negative manner, as shown on page 35. To maintain good relations and ongoing trade, it is usually wise to give the customer the benefit of the doubt, whenever possible. Consider any precedents that may be set by whatever it is you decide to do, though.

answering a complaint, positive response

'Hello, Mr Patel. It's Ivan Lucas at DDX. I'm returning your call as promised.'

'Oh, hello, Mr Lucas. Thank you for calling back.'

'I've looked into this matter and can confirm that your cheque was credited to another account. Human error, I'm afraid. I apologise to you for this, and have arranged for the amount to be credited to your account today. We've initiated procedures to ensure this doesn't reoccur. Again, please accept my apologies for this. I'm sorry.'

comments

1. Few managers wish to accept that a complaint about products, services or an employee is justified, and are even less enthusiastic about apologising for it, but sometimes it needs to be done. On the telephone, a complaint can at least be resolved informally, without extensive, on-the-record correspondence and documentation.
2. Try to keep the conversation fairly short, albeit friendly – you do not want to dwell on your company's weaknesses, however temporary they are. Acknowledge what has happened and apologise for it, but without labouring the reasons why – the customer really isn't that interested. Explain what you have done to ensure that the matter does not arise again, which is always a concern for a customer who is thinking of buying from you in the future.
3. If the customer's requested course of action or remedy is fair and reasonable, it is sensible to agree to this. You should carry it out as soon as possible (if it is not

already being attended to). If not – perhaps the customer wants a damaged, year-old product replaced by a brand new one – then a compromise should be suggested, such as a free-of-charge repair. Err on the generous side if you are at fault, especially if you wish to retain their custom. End the conversation by apologising again.

4. Apologies should be kept in proportion to the significance of what has happened – something fairly minor, such as a clerical oversight with limited repercussions or a quickly replaced, faulty product sold by you warrants a sincere but relatively brief apology. These mistakes are unfortunate but do happen from time to time. Most people will recognise that. If you deal fairly with them, that's the end of the matter. More significant errors that cause loss of business or damage to someone's reputation will need to be dealt with more formally in writing and at a higher level.

answering a complaint, negative response

'Hello, Mrs Jones. This is Kim Bakewell at Durbridge Brothers. I'm returning your call about the CD system.'

'About time. What are you doing about it, then?'

'Well, I'm returning your call as promised. We've now looked at the system in the workshop and think the mechanism has broken because it appears to have been shut manually rather than automatically by pressing the button.'

'What do you mean? Are you saying it's my fault? Is that what you mean?'

'We're sorry you're unhappy, Mrs Jones, but it does seem to have been closed manually, rather than automatically by pressing the button.'

'Well, that's disgusting, that is. So it's my fault. Typical. Who says it has to be closed automatically?'

'It is stated on the first page of the instruction booklet that came with the system...'

'I never got one.'

'... and there is a sticker on the front of the mechanism that states it too.'

'... Well, it's stupid, anyway... '

comments

1. Evidently, rejecting a customer's complaint over the telephone is a tough task. You can prepare what you are going to say initially, but invariably you will then have to deal with an unpredictable response, which is difficult to do. More often than not, they will become angry and may well threaten legal action.
2. In your opening comments, it is sensible to acknowledge the matter. Then reject the complaint as politely and as diplomatically as you can, explaining your reasons as succinctly as possible. Try to adopt non-confrontational language, avoiding a 'them and us' attitude. Avoid using the 'you' word, as in 'you seem to have done this'. Instead, make it non-specific. 'It seems to have...' Sound sympathetic, but be firm.
3. If the complaint was made sincerely but was misguided – perhaps the customer has been using the item incorrectly – then, hopefully, they will accept your comments. As often as not, the response will be a heated one and you should be ready for this,

remaining calm, repeating and explaining briefly your position as necessary, whatever is said. Ideally, you will let them work through their anger until they see reason and agree with you – thus, future trade may be a possibility.

chasing a debt, first call

'Hello, this is Edward Hopkins from the Accounts Department at Addington–Davies. I'm ringing about invoice 443 dated 7 March for £389.95. This was due for payment by 13 April, but we don't seem to have a record of its payment. Can you tell me if it's been paid, please?'

'Um... I'm not sure. I think that's been paid... Hold on... No, not yet... Leave it with me, and I'll sort it out.'

'Can you tell me when you will send us a cheque?'

'Er... well, I... I'll get something off to you this week.'

'So you'll post a cheque for £389.95 to us by Friday?'

'Yes, yes I will.'

'Thank you. Please would you mark the envelope for my attention – Edward Hopkins in the Accounts Department.'

comments

1. Sending letters to chase an overdue bill or outstanding account is often of only limited use, simply because they are easy to ignore (at least until further supplies of stock are halted or legal action commences). Telephone calls can be more effective because they have to be dealt with on-the-sport.
2. In your first call, you should begin by introducing yourself to whoever is responsible for making payment

and specifying the key facts – the invoice number, date, amount and date of expected payment, for example. Always have those facts ready. Then ask politely if it has been paid. Bear in mind that payment may just have been sent or genuinely have been overlooked, so do not jump automatically to conclusions. Give them the benefit of the doubt, not least because you want to remain on good terms with them and retain their custom.

3. If they say that payment has just been made – and remember that you have no reason to suspect otherwise at this point – obtain details of what was sent, how and when, so that you can estimate when it will arrive. Ignore whatever doubts you may have and thank them for this information. Do not apologise for troubling them, as this suggests that you have been unreasonable.
4. Alternatively, they may admit that payment has not been made, perhaps for a very good reason, or that it has simply been overlooked. Again, accept this explanation but, as in the example, press them to tell you what is being sent and when so that you can monitor the situation more easily. On occasions, the recipient of your call may say that they are experiencing financial difficulties. Hopefully, you can come to a payment arrangement with them, as shown on pages 42 and 44.
5. If the customer is trying to delay or avoid making payment to you, their typical response, as suggested in the example, will be one of vague promises and assurances. In such circumstances, you need to get them to specify exactly when payment will be made, how and where, as relevant. This focuses their mind, indicates that you will not let the matter drift, and provides you with a deadline that you can then use to follow up the matter further, and relatively quickly. And look out for that payment. If it doesn't arrive when expected (allowing a day or two's grace), follow up again.

chasing a debt, second call

'Mr Berry, it's Penny Milner from Abacom's accounts section. One of my assistants spoke to you last Monday regarding your unpaid invoice 798 for £1,564.97, due for payment on 31 October. I understood that you were posting a cheque to us that day, but we haven't received it yet. Have you sent it?'

'It should have gone, but it didn't. Our systems went down that day and caused all sorts of trouble.'

'When will you send it?'

'I'll get on to it today.'

'We do need to receive a cheque by Friday at the latest. Unfortunately, it is company policy to suspend supplies to those firms whose accounts are more than 45 days overdue, and you will come into this category after Friday. Will you send a cheque by then?'

'Yes, I'll see what I can do.'

comments

1. When chasing money by phone, you need to be polite but persistent. If the payment does not arrive as promised, then, after allowing two days' grace in case of postal delays or whatever, you must make a follow-up call, however embarrassing you may find this to be. It may be a good idea to arrange for someone more senior to make the second call, to show how seriously the situation is regarded. You need to create the sense that this matter is being pursued, fairly but firmly.
2. Whatever your doubts about the person or the firm, remain courteous and neutral during the conversation. Steer clear of expressing your doubts and avoid

making sarcastic comments, veiled threats and voicing other unpleasantries. You should always seek to maintain a fair and reasonable image in the business community, which is essential if you trade with that person's or firm's fellow traders.

3. Be firm, setting a deadline for receiving payment and stating clearly what will happen if it is not met. This should be something definite but reversible, such as the suspension of credit facilities, rather than being final and permanent. For example, closing the account does not encourage payment and effectively terminates the relationship, which may be your loss, too. They would then have no incentive to pay up.
4. Once the deadline has passed, you must be willing to carry out what you said would be done on that precise date, otherwise, you will be perceived to be weak and uncertain, and your chances of being paid will be diminished. Notify them (by letter) that you have carried out that action, so they know you are serious.

chasing a debt, third call

'Mr Buerk? My name's Suzanne Chang. I'm the Accounts Manager at BDS and I'm phoning with regard to invoice 214 for £876.88. This was due for payment on 30 June. We have not received your payment.'

'... Haven't you?'

'No. We telephoned you on 8 and 18 July and asked you to make payment. You said on both occasions that you would forward a cheque in settlement within a few days. We haven't received that cheque.'

'Really?'

'I'm telephoning now to say that we must have a cheque for £876.88 here no later than this coming Friday, when the invoice will be 60 days old. If it is not received then, it is company policy to issue a county court summons on that day to recover the sum, plus expenses. Will you send a cheque for this amount by then?'

comments

1. Sometimes, the temporary suspension of credit facilities, supplies or the like does not have the desired effect and it becomes obvious that you are not going to be paid unless you take much firmer action – for example, you will have to pass the account over to a debt collection agency or issue a county court summons. In such circumstances, you need to be seen to be acting in a fair and reasonable manner, giving the debtor sufficient warning of your intentions, and an opportunity either to make payment or to come up with an agreeable compromise of staggered, smaller ones.
2. This telephone conversation should follow a set pattern. Begin by referring to the invoice you are chasing – its number, date, amount and when it was due to be settled. Then refer to your previous calls – dates, what you asked them to do and what they promised to do. State that this does not appear to have been done. Indicate what you need to receive, by when and what will happen if you do not. Ask for payment.
3. As with your second chasing call, as shown on page 39, you need to be polite, but persistent, at all times. To indicate how seriously the matter is viewed, it can be a good idea to have this call made by a senior person within the department or firm. Follow up the conversation with a letter specifying the main points

again. Be prepared to follow through with the stated action – for example, issuing a summons.

the request for a delayed payment schedule, positive response

'312. David Jones speaking.'

'Hello, David. It's Carl Booker from Doves of Derewich... We're experiencing some unexpected but temporary cash-flow problems at the moment – one of our overseas customers is being rather slow in paying us. We're not able to settle your invoice 5678 for £3,650.56 that is due shortly. Would you accept payments over three months?'

'Hold on, let me check... Yes, we can do that as a one-off on this occasion. Let's see... Can you let me have a cheque for £1,309.50 in the next couple of days, along with two post-dated cheques for £1,309 for 13 March and 13 April? We'll hold these and present them on those dates.'

'I can get the first cheque off to you tonight, but I'd prefer to date the other cheques on the last day of March and April. Is that okay?'

'... Yes, that will be acceptable.'

'While I'm on the phone to you, what's the position about our outstanding orders 921 and 934? Will you release these?'

'... As you know, we're not able to send anything out if it would take a customer over their credit limit or if there is an outstanding balance on the account... 921 is due to go out tomorrow and will do as you'll still be within your limit, and invoice 6023 isn't due until next week. When will you be able to pay that?'

'I'll add it to the last payment in April, if that's okay.'

'Yes... I'll work out what's due once I've checked with despatch and put this in writing to you today with an sae for you to send me the cheques by return...'

comments

1. Ideally, customers who are experiencing financial problems will contact you at an early stage, before you start to chase payment, or they will at least acknowledge these difficulties as soon as you get in touch with them. If they do, this is probably a good sign, as it implies that it is a temporary situation that is being dealt with, and that the customer wishes to retain a sound working relationship with you, now and in the future.
2. Mindful of this, it is usually sensible to agree with any reasonable offer that is made to you or to seek a compromise if it is not. As a sign of good faith, ask for the first payment to be forwarded straight away and for subsequent payments to be made by post-dated cheques which you will hold until they are due for presentation. This increases your chances of being paid fully and on time. Obviously, it is up to you to decide whether you want to supply more goods to them during this period of extended credit. Often, this is unwise, but you will need to handle the refusal carefully.
3. Follow up this conversation with written confirmation of what was agreed and enclose a stamped addressed envelope for the first payment and post-dated cheques to be sent to you by return, as appropriate. Be very clear about payment dates and amounts, monitoring them as necessary. Chase any that are not made, as shown on pages 37, 39 and 40. You need to be fair but firm when dealing with such a situation.

the request for a delayed payment proposal, negative response

'So, as I say, it's very, very tough at the moment. So can we come to some sort of arrangement for paying this bill?'

'What exactly did you have in mind, Mr Warnock?'

'We reckon we're probably going to be out of the mire in two to three months – say, November at the latest. Can we settle up then?'

'No, I'm sorry, Mr Warnock, but we can't afford to wait that long. We've our own cash-flow to consider. We'd be prepared to accept payment in three equal instalments. If you'll send us a cheque for the first payment today, and two post-dated cheques for next month and the month after, we would be agreeable to that.'

'Oh... I see. Well, no... no, I don't think we can manage that...'

'We do need to have some sort of payment straight away with the balance payable over the next two months, Mr Warnock. Alternatively, we will need to think about collecting our goods back from you or pursuing payment of the debt. Perhaps you'd like to think things over and come back to me with your suggestions... I'm in all day...'

comments

1. Sometimes, the proposed repayment schedule on an overdue bill or account will be unacceptable, with lower payments being spread over a longer period than you would like. In such a situation you will need to negotiate a compromise deal. If you are successful,

keep a close watch on repayments, as these are likely to fall behind and will need to be pursued. If you cannot reach agreement, you may decide to start chasing the full amount straight away, as seen on pages 37, 39 and 40.

2. Keep the conversation brief and to the point – there is nothing to be gained by extending it. Listen to the offer and consider it. If you decide to reject it – and it is worth mulling over the consequences of this before going any further – then say so, and give a concise reason for it. Suggest an alternative and come to an agreement, as relevant. If this is impossible ask them to think it over and point out what will happen next if payments are not made.

calling a customer who has not used their account for some time

'Bernard Kemp.'

'Hello, Mr Kemp, this is Sarah Wells at K-8. I work in the Sales department. You may remember that we met at the King's Court exhibition in the spring – I was with Harry Andrews.'

'Yes, yes I do. How are you?'

'I'm fine, thank you. I've been asked to compile our sales statistics for the year and I noticed that you haven't used your account for a while. I just wondered why that was?'

'Oh, well... to be honest, I've been buying a lot of stock from Websters. They're a bit cheaper than you.'

'I see. Well, since you last bought from us, we have introduced a new discount structure for early settlement and bulk purchases. If you take advantage of these, you will save a considerable sum. Also, we have increased our product range by more than 50 per cent and are now the largest on-site stockist in the county...'

comments

1. Sales-orientated companies have systems and procedures in place to highlight those customers who have not used their accounts for some time and who do not respond to mailings of sales catalogues, forthcoming offers, and the like. In such circumstances, a telephone call may be made to ascertain the reasons and, assuming they are still trading, to encourage them to start buying from you again.
2. Get off to a good opening by establishing a rapport quickly. You may be able to do this by using their first name if you were previously on friendly terms, or by addressing them more formally to show respect. Make them feel important by having their facts and figures at your fingertips, and referring to these.
3. Ask them politely why they have not used their account for a while, avoiding the word 'stopped' or anything similar as it sounds rather final. Put the question in as neutral a manner as you can, without sounding reproachful or apologetic, which suggests that you think they have experienced problems in their dealings with you. Don't draw attention to your shortcomings, especially as they may not have experienced any.
4. Follow their lead in the conversation; if they have faced a problem, listen carefully to what they say, get the facts, promise to look into it, do so and respond promptly, as illustrated on pages 30, 32 and 34. Frequently, the reason they have not bought from you lately is that they have been purchasing goods else-

where, from a supplier who offers cheaper items and/or better services. If so, concentrate on promoting what you can offer them.

5. Conclude by encouraging them to order from you again, perhaps by offering to send your latest catalogue, by arranging for a representative to call to demonstrate new products or by referring to a special (limited) offer. If necessary, it may be worth offering them some sort of special, one-off deal to entice them back to you.

calling a customer who has closed their account

'Mr Powell, my name is Andrea Bailey. I'm the Sales Director at TPG Maslow. I've just been passed your letter closing your account. I'm really sorry about this and wonder if you can tell me about your experiences with us?'

'Where do I start? It's been one thing after another. First of all, I didn't get any of my orders sent...'

'Go on...'

'... After that, I started getting orders I didn't want...'

'Tell me about it, Mr Powell...'

'... and finally – and worst of all – I started receiving nasty letters from you for goods I knew nothing about...'

'Thank you for spending time telling me all about this, Mr Powell. I want to apologise to you. We've fallen below the high standards we set for ourselves. The vast majority of our customers are always very satisfied with what we do, but occasionally problems do arise, which we try to deal with promptly. In this case, the difficulty occurred because your business has the same name and a similar postcode to another firm in Grimsdale and that created problems. We've now amended our computer records so that this cannot happen again.'

'Oh, I see... computers. Well that doesn't surprise me. They're often more trouble than they're worth.'

'What I'd like to do, Mr Powell, is to ask you to give us another try. We recognise we've been at fault and would like to write off the outstanding balance on the account because of this. Let us try again and show you what we can do for you...'

comments

1. Often, a phone call to someone who has made a specific point of closing their account can achieve better results than one made to a person who has not used their account for some time, as illustrated on page 45. Typically, the account will have been closed in anger or disappointment, and if you can address and resolve this difficulty, the chances of trading together again are quite high.
2. Begin by acknowledging that the account has been closed, indicate regret and ask them if they can tell you why. If they have already provided this information, perhaps in a letter – and you should therefore know about it (having done your pre-call research) – you could ask them instead to elaborate on it. Most customers will welcome the opportunity to air their grievances.
3. Indicate that you are listening to what they are saying by murmuring 'yes', 'go on' and 'tell me more', when relevant. Obtain all the information you need to investigate the matter by asking who–what–when–where–why–how? questions, as appropriate. If necessary,

promise to investigate the matter and come back to them at an agreed time, which you should then do to resolve the complaint, as seen on pages 30, 32 and 34.

4. If you can deal with the problem immediately – because you have studied a letter and investigated it prior to the call, you should attempt to do so. In most cases, the customer wants an apology, a brief explanation and assurances, backed up by some form of supporting evidence, that it will not happen again. Depending on the seriousness of the matter and how angry or disappointed the customer is, you may also need to offer some kind of special deal (discounts, 2-for-1 offers, etc) to bring them back to you.

3

talking to suppliers

It is not always easy to converse with suppliers, not least because you often have different needs and wants, and expectations of each other. They want you to pay in advance; you require credit facilities. They cannot deliver goods until next month; you need them next week – and so on. As often as not, you seem to be constantly at odds with each other. Difficult calls of this nature can be grouped in three ways:

- those involving the purchase of goods and services, at the best price, and on the most favourable terms and conditions;
- those where you are trying to resolve problems – for example concerning overdue, damaged or faulty goods;
- those where you attempt to get a better deal, returning unsold products, increasing or extending credit facilities, and the like.

the call from a sales representative

'... Now, I'm in a position to be able to do you a favour here, Martin. At the moment, we're offering a free, no obligation demonstration of the "Syrita" in the comfort of your own home. But this offer is only available until...'

'To be frank, Miss Halliday, I'm really very busy. If you put a sales catalogue and a price list in the post to me though, I'll take a look and come back to you if I wish to take the matter further. I don't have time to discuss this, nor be visited by you or your representative.'

'Okay, I'll tell you what I'll do. I'll send you a catalogue and order form by first-class post tonight and give you a call on Friday to go through it with you.'

'No, thank you. Send me the details and I'll call you if I want to go any further.'

comments

1. Some calls from sales representatives will be welcome; you know these people, are pleased to hear about their products, services and developments and will wish to buy from them. These calls will probably not pose problems for you. However, other calls may be made to you on a speculative basis by representatives you do not know; and you might be unfamiliar with their goods and services too. You are unsure whether you are interested in taking the matter further or not. These conversations are more difficult to handle.
2. To begin with, be aware of the caller's objectives. Often, they will be trying to make an immediate sale over the telephone. If they cannot do that, they will almost certainly seek to arrange to visit you in person

themselves, or to send an agent around. Failing that, they will wish to forward some literature – for example a sales brochure and an order form. At the very least, they will want to make a follow-up call to you on an agreed date during which they will start this process again.

3. Next, you must decide what you want from this conversation. Perhaps you do not wish to talk at the moment, preferring them to call back at a more convenient time. If you are potentially interested, you may be well advised to seek the information you need to make a decision over the phone – prices, terms, conditions, and so on – rather than agreeing to a time-consuming meeting with a pushy salesperson. Alternatively, you might wish to have the details sent to you for consideration. Know what you want and what you do not want – a personal visit, chasing phone calls for a decision, and so on.
4. The key to success with this type of call is to be specific, firm and to stay in control. Set out what you do and do not want. Don't let the salesperson talk you into agreeing something you are unhappy with. Be prepared to break into their sales pitch, repeating your position if necessary, as seen in the example conversation. Work to *your* agenda, not theirs.

the call from a market researcher

'Good morning. I'm conducting a survey on energy efficiency. Do you have two minutes to give me your opinions?'

'Possibly. Can you tell me who you are, what company you represent and the telephone number you're calling from, please?'

'... Yes, of course. My name's Justine. I work for a company called Instalex.'

'And your phone number?'

'... It's 01121 132321. I'll only take up a minute or two of your time. Can you tell me how you heat your premises?'

'Yes, I can. But before I do, can you just tell me what your business does exactly, please?'

comments

1. Sometimes, you will receive calls from people who claim to be conducting market research, and who want to know your thoughts and opinions on a range of issues. You may be happy to be interviewed and to provide this information, but it is sensible to check that the person is who they say they are, and not a salesperson who is consequently going to try to talk you into buying something.
2. A genuine caller should start the conversation by telling you the name and telephone number of the market research company they represent – if they do not, ask for it. Should you have any doubts about the caller, request more information about their firm – its areas of activity and whether it belongs to any professional bodies. It should be a member of the Market Research Society.
3. If you still remain doubtful, ask them to call back at an agreed time. Then dial 100 and ask the operator for 'Freefone Market Research Society'. This is a free call and can be made to check the status of the company concerned. If the society confirms that it is a bona fide research organisation, you can go ahead and take part in the survey should you wish to do so. If it is not verified, you may decide not to, since this suggests that it may be a person or organisation that is attempting to sell to you using rather dubious methods.

the call from a persistent sales representative

'Hi, Gemma. It's Paul Braithwaite here at B–Mex. I sent you our sales brochure as you requested. Have you received it yet?'

'Hello, Mr Braithwaite. Thank you for calling. I haven't looked at your brochure yet, but I will do so shortly and will then call you if I wish to take the matter further.'

'Oh, that's fine. I just wanted to check you'd received it. What was it you were interested in?'

'As I say, I haven't looked at the brochure yet. If I see anything that interests me, I'll phone you.'

'Can I draw your attention to the special offers that we have available for a limited period? Do you have the brochure there?'

'No, I'll look at it later and then come back to you if I want to proceed. Now, if you'll excuse me, I am very busy.'

comments

1. Some sales representatives and research companies from the telemarketing industry are very persistent, especially if you allow them to be. If you receive a further unwanted call, it will probably be because you were not firm enough during your original conversation with them (see page 51). So you need to handle this conversation well if you are to avoid the situation being repeated.
2. Thank them for calling, then make it very clear what is and is not going to happen – typically, you will be in touch with them if you decide to pursue the matter, but

you do not want to be called again before that, or to be visited by sales agents, or whatever.

3. Do not respond to their statements or questions, as this enables them to take control of the conversation and leads it where they want to go. Inevitably, you then find yourself agreeing to something you do not really want, often because you are too polite to say 'no'. Stay in charge of the conversation simply by repeating your position, albeit in a variety of ways.

stopping unwanted sales calls

'As I say, Mr Hawkins, I am not interested in your goods or services, and do not wish to take this matter any further. Please do not call me again.'

'Let me just send you our new catalogue when it's available next month. We've some special offers that may interest you.'

'No, thank you. I am not interested at all. Please do not contact me again. I'm very busy and have to go now, so if you'll excuse me. Goodbye.'

comments

1. There may come a time with some persistent sales representatives when you decide that you need to put a stop to their incoming calls. They just won't take 'no' for an answer. With a telemarketing organisation, you might receive calls from several representatives all working independently from the same list, which can be frustrating. Again, you may wish to stop these calls.
2. If you are receiving calls from sales agents you know, the best approach is simply to state that you are not

interested in their products or services and ask them to stop calling you. Be brief and firm; do not allow yourself to be drawn into a conversation. As in the example, conclude the conversation if necessary. In most cases, this should be sufficient. If not, you will need to repeat the conversation and follow it with a letter of complaint to the firm.

3. Your approach to unsolicited callers from telemarketing companies should be the same, and you can reduce further the volume of calls of this nature by registering with the Telephone Preference Service. This is a free service set up by the telemarketing and telecommunications industries that enables consumers to have their telephone numbers removed from telemarketing lists. If you are a British Telecom customer, call 0800 398 893 for more information, or collect a TPS registration form from your nearest BT shop. Alternatively, get in touch with your own network operator for contact details and advice.

enquiring about goods and services

'... So can you tell me the price of a Statton Deluxe model, please?'

'Yes. We can offer you a special price on that, but for a limited period only. Can I take your name and details, please?'

'No, thank you. At the moment, I'd just like to know the price. I'll then think it over and come back to you.'

'We'd be very happy to arrange for one of our advisers to give you a free-of-charge, no obligation demonstration if you'll let me have your details...'

'No, thank you. Not at the moment. Would you like to give me a price? If you can't, then I'll try elsewhere.'

'Hold on, I'll check it for you...'

comments

1. This type of call can be a tricky one. On the one hand, you want to obtain sufficient information over the phone to decide whether you want to take the matter further or not. On the other hand, the recipient of your call is often keen to force through an immediate sale or at least to secure some form of commitment from you that you may not want to give. So try to sound calm and matter-of-fact, rather than interested or even enthusiastic, which will only encourage them more.
2. Ask precisely what you want to know – prices, specifications, lead times, trading terms and conditions, or whatever. Keep the questions brief and to the point, repeating them if necessary – typically, when the other person uses a question to launch into a sales pitch. Do not respond to their questions and requests, and make it clear that you do not want to place an order now or to be visited by their sales representative, and so on. Say what you want and will do next – for example, request sales literature to study, followed by an order if you decide to proceed. Remember, the golden rule here is: be firm!

requesting a discount

'Our initial order would be about £500 and we can pay cash on collection of the goods from your warehouse. After that, I'd expect to take about the same amount each month and could pay cash when we picked up the orders. What discount can you give us off your list prices for this?'

'We'd normally offer 5 per cent for cash on collection, Mr Davies.'

'We're really looking for something closer to 10 per cent. Obviously, if we can buy from you with a reasonable discount, we'll be able to afford more of your goods. Also, by paying cash straight away, I'm sure that would help your cash-flow. Can you improve on 5 per cent for this amount of business?'

'Well... perhaps we could go up to 7½ per cent for you...'

comments

1. When ordering or buying goods or services, it is always sensible to ask for a discount, whether for payment in advance, a bulk buy or simply because you want to pay a lower price! If you don't ask, you probably won't get anything, or at least not as much as you could receive if you requested it.
2. Your approach should be keen, but cautious. You want to buy, but can only do so if the price is agreeable. Set out what you want to purchase, and when and how you intend to pay for it. Next, you can either indicate the type of discount you are looking for or ask what is available, consequently suggesting a larger one, if necessary.
3. It can be a good idea to say how such a discount will benefit you and them. Concentrate on the positive reasons why they should agree to your request – a discount will enable you to order more from them, paying up-front will improve their cash-flow, and so on. Focus in particular on how they will gain from it. As with all calls of this nature, say what's in it for them.
4. Avoid the negative reasons why they should agree to a discount – 'If you don't, I'll take my custom else-

where', and the like – since these sound like threats, which are rarely received favourably. Also, avoid bluffing, as you may find that your bluff may be called – 'Okay, go elsewhere, then'. Never make a statement unless you are prepared to follow it through.

asking for credit terms

'So we'd expect to spend £1,000 or so with you to start with, which should give us a decent range of your goods on display and in stock. All going well, we'd then be looking to order approximately £250 to £300 worth of items each month. Can you offer us a credit account?'

'What sort of limit did you have in mind, Miss Charles?'

'Say £1,500 to begin with; we could then see how that worked out. Obviously, we can give you first-class references, both bank and trade.'

'Let me have a couple of trade names and addresses to begin with.'

'You can approach Leah Bishop at Bartrams and Nigel Jones at Bettacom. I'd be very happy for you to phone them if you'd like to. Shall I give you their numbers?'

'Yes, that would be useful...'

comments

1. It is advisable to request credit facilities at the beginning of a trading relationship, whether you intend to use them or not. If you ask for them later – perhaps after you have been paying on a cash-with-order or cash-on-collection basis for some time – this could be interpreted as a sign that you are experiencing

financial difficulties. Not surprisingly, this would be a cause for rejecting your request.

2. Set out what you expect to buy and ask for credit terms, suggesting a limit that you could work within comfortably, and that is likely to prove acceptable to the supplier. Be ready to provide details of reputable, well-known people or organisations that can supply references about your financial and commercial standing. Usually, you will be asked for your banker's details, and two other suppliers with whom you trade. Inviting this supplier to phone your trade referees should inspire confidence in your status. A banker's reference will be taken up by their bank.

chasing overdue products or services, agreeable delivery date

'... I'm 'phoning about our order number 62 for 12 AZ-55s, dated 7 September. We'd normally expect delivery by the end of the month, but haven't yet received it. Can you tell me when it will be delivered?'

'I'd have to check on that for you; I know they've had one or two problems... one moment, please... yes, there have been some difficulties getting the parts in from Italy. There's been a strike there...'

'Can you give me a delivery date?'

'We're expecting something in next week and will then despatch as soon as we can.'

'So if the parts arrive next week when will you despatch to me?'

'Some time the following week, all being well. We're quite quick when we get going.'

'Can you make a note on our account that we do need to have this order delivered no later than the 23rd of this month? Otherwise, we won't be able to sell them on to our customers...'

comments

1. It is always difficult to know what to do if goods or services are not supplied at the agreed time – whether you should wait for them or try to obtain replacements from another source. In the first instance, it is a good idea to make a telephone call to the prospective supplier to check on the current situation.
2. Open the conversation by referring to the order – its number, date, contents, and when and why you expected to receive delivery of the goods – for example, because goods normally arrive within three weeks, you expected them by that date. Then ask them when delivery will be made.
3. Often, the recipient of your call will offer a long and meandering reason for the delay, and be vague and uncertain about what is happening. You may need to cut into this with a direct question like 'When will delivery be made to me?' Clearly, you need a definite answer so that you can decide what to do – whether to wait or to go elsewhere.
4. If you receive a firm date, you can make your decision. If an approximate date is given, you should try to get them to estimate as closely as possible. Should you agree to wait, it may be a good idea to set a deadline for delivery, giving a brief reason for this – typically, because you have customers waiting, too. You may wish to state what you will do if this deadline is not

met, but only if you are prepared to follow this through. Once the deadline has arrived, ring to check what is happening, and then go elsewhere or take alternative action, as necessary.

chasing overdue products or services, disagreeable delivery date

'... Obviously we'll forward the goods to you as soon as we can.'

'Can you give me a despatch date, please?'

'No, but as soon as we have them we'll send them on.'

'Can you at least give me an approximate date?'

'No, I'm sorry; we are doing our best, and will forward them at the earliest opportunity.'

'In that case, I'm sorry too but I think I'll have to cancel this order on this occasion. If we don't get the goods in by Friday, we won't be able to sell them on ourselves. So if that's not achievable, we'll have to cancel...'

comments

1. Sometimes, when chasing overdue products or services, the recipient of your call will be vague and unsure of the likely delivery date or, when pressed, will state a date that is too late for you. In such circumstances, it is probably best to take your custom elsewhere, at least on this occasion.
2. If you cannot wait for this delayed delivery, then you should say so, explaining your reasons as briefly and

as politely as you can and indicating, if appropriate, that you hope you can do business together again at some point in the future.

3. Whether you are waiting for a delayed delivery, as shown on page 60, or are taking your business elsewhere, it is advisable to follow a call of this nature with a letter confirming what was said and agreed. Hopefully, this will help to avoid any subsequent confusion or misunderstandings.

rejecting damaged goods

'Despatch. Rick speaking. How can I help you?'

'Hello, my name is Robin Burns, at H. C. Broomfields in Rotherby, Yorkshire. I'm telephoning to acknowledge receipt of your delivery 6497 that arrived this morning, and to inform you that a box of RD-55s is damaged.'

'Hang on... I'll make a note of this.'

'The problem is that we can't use these items and do need replacements quickly so we can fulfil our own customer orders. Can you deliver replacements and collect the damaged items by the end of the week?'

'I don't know. I'll have to find out and call you back. What's your number?'

'It's 01212 212323. We do need this to be sorted out by Friday. If we don't get them by then, we'll lose our orders, which means we'll have to cancel this one with you.'

comments

1. It is common business practice to accept a delivery of boxed goods as seen and to sign for them before they

are unpacked and inspected individually. On those occasions when they are subsequently checked and found to be damaged, you should telephone the supplier immediately to inform them of the situation.

2. State what was delivered, when, and explain briefly what is wrong with it. Quote order numbers, delivery numbers, and so on, as relevant. Keep this short and to the point.
3. Say what you want them to do about it – typically, to collect and replace the damaged goods as soon as possible. If appropriate – perhaps because you have your own customer orders to fulfil – specify a date by which this action must be carried out. It is important that this is achievable.
4. Indicate what you will do if they have not complied with your request by the stated time – for example, you will (reluctantly) take your custom elsewhere (on this occasion). Again, be careful to set a realistic length of time, otherwise you might be forced to follow through when perhaps you would prefer not to.
5. It is a wise idea to follow up this conversation with a letter confirming the main points – fax it through to them for greater emphasis. Too often, problems of this nature are not attended to as quickly as you would like them to be. A faxed letter may be of some assistance in this situation.
6. In future, always try to open boxed goods on delivery. Some unscrupulous firms send out faulty goods and then claim they must have been damaged after delivery! Alternatively, sign the receipt as 'received, but unopened'. This provides you with some legal protection.

making a complaint, accepted

'... We bought it in February for £665 from your sales representative, Wendy McLeish, who brought it in, installed it and went through how to work it. She then left us an operations manual, which we've read and followed.'

'So what's the problem, Mr Reisz?'

'To be blunt, it's unreliable, and doesn't give us the service we'd expect from it. Wendy has had to repair it on three out of her last four calls – in March, April and June. I'm sure you'll have copies of her record sheets available to refer to.'

'Right, yes. I can get hold of those, no problem. What do you want us to do then?'

'Well, I appreciate it's second-hand, and we paid a good price, so I'd like Wendy to collect it on her next visit and take it back to the workshop for a free-of-charge overhaul. If you can let us have a replacement model while it's away and Wendy can return our reconditioned unit on her next call, we'd be happy with that. We could then see how it worked after that.'

'Hold on, I'll need to have a word... Yes, we can do that. Let's get something arranged now...'

comments

1. It can be difficult to complain – if you are too soft, you may not be treated seriously. You'll be seen as a 'soft touch'. If you are too hard and/or complain too often, relations may be harmed. You'll be viewed as a troublemaker. Whatever the nature of the complaint – faulty goods, poor service, a rude employee or whatever – it should follow a set procedure.

2. Provide brief background comments about the matter – for example, what was bought, when, how much was paid, and how you have used it. Make your complaint, giving the reason for your dissatisfaction and supporting it with facts and figures – for example, the dates and details of faults with the product. State what you want to be done and by when – typically, a refund or a replacement item within 7–14 days.
3. If they are agreeable to your request, it is sensible to forward a fax confirming the agreement as soon as the conversation has ended. Should they want to compromise, you need to decide how far you are willing to move from your position. Be aware of your legal rights when deciding this. Again, follow up this conversation with a fax, setting down the main points of the compromise agreement.

making a complaint, rejected

'... No, I'm sorry, Mr Stamford, but I can't agree to that.'

'Why is that?'

'Well you've had the use of the equipment for the best part of a year now and have had plenty of opportunities to complain before now, and haven't done. We do get a lot of customers bringing back items when a newer model is being launched, and they try to get us to replace the old one with the new one.'

'That may well be so, but it isn't the case here. As I say, we were unaware of any problems until last Monday, when it stopped working. Batty's engineer looked at it, and has confirmed that the RX-22 component has burnt out because it has overloaded due to faulty wiring. As these components are no longer being manufactured, the equipment cannot be used as it is, and as the fault was caused by your firm, I think it is fair and reasonable for us to request a replacement from you.'

'But you've had the use of it, haven't you?'

'I think that's beside the point. We do want to resolve this matter amicably and between ourselves, but if we cannot do this, we will need to take the matter further in order to obtain a replacement or a refund. We do need to sort this out quickly as we use this equipment on a day-to-day basis. Perhaps I can ask you to think things over and come back to me; but I must stress that I will need to know your response by Friday, if the matter is not to go any further.'

comments

1. From time to time, you will raise a complaint about a supplier's goods, services or employees, and this will be rejected. It is important that you stay calm and in control when this happens as this type of situation can easily and quickly degenerate into a heated argument, from which no one will benefit at all.
2. If the recipient of your call refuses to accept your request – for a replacement product, improved services, an apology or whatever – you should repeat the key facts of the matter again. Then specify what you intend to do if the situation is not resolved satisfactorily, by a set date. Be prepared to carry out whatever you say you will do, and do so on that specific date, otherwise your credibility will be damaged and your prospects for a favourable settlement will be much reduced.
3. Do send a letter to this person after the conversation has ended, specifying what was said, what you want and by when, and what you will do if your fair and reasonable request is not fulfilled by that date.

querying a bill

'Good morning; my name is Kate Baines, the manager at Cooper Greene. Our account number with you is CO 001. Can you bring our account details up on your screen, please?'

'One moment... yes, there we are. Can you confirm your address, please? The postcode will do.'

'It's IP11 0YS... We've just received this month's statement, which I need to query. Can you get it on screen?'

'Yes, I have that in front of me now.'

'Okay... we received a delivery of RN-222s costing £1,450.45 on 2 September... These relate to invoice IN-2934 dated 1 September. Some of the goods were faulty. You uplifted these and issued us with credit note CN-434 for £397.94 on 5 September. This isn't showing on the statement.... When you picked up the faulty goods, you delivered some replacements that cost £288.98. But you issued invoice IN-3003 for £397.94 and this incorrect figure is showing on the statement. Because of this, the statement shows us being over our credit limit, which means a stop will apply to our account. Can you help?'

comments

1. If you want to telephone to query a bill or a series of debits and credits, payments and miscellaneous charges on a statement, there are various guidelines that you should adhere to. Before you call, check, double-check and then check again that your calculations are absolutely correct. Make sure that you speak to someone who has the authority to look into and resolve the problem. Have all the necessary documentation to hand when you make that call.

2. Keep the call as simple as possible. Introduce yourself and say why you are calling – for example, to notify them that an invoice is incorrect, a payment has not been credited to your account, or whatever. Provide a brief, simplified summary of the facts. Pause between each key fact to give the other person time to absorb it and/or make a note of it. If you give all the facts in one go, they'll feel bombarded, and may react negatively. The recipient of your call may then want to investigate the matter, and phone you back. Be ready to provide detailed information – dates, reference numbers, amounts, and so on – as and when requested. Follow up this call with written confirmation of the facts and figures, and what was agreed – for example, the issue of a credit note. Sometimes, conversations are subsequently overlooked and not acted upon as promised. A fax and/or a letter helps.

asking to return unsold goods

'... To tell you the truth, Jacques, I think I was so taken with your new range when I was looking at them that I got a bit carried away, and over-ordered. They're terrific items, but I've just taken too many of them. Can I return some?... perhaps those still in their original boxes. They're in tip-top condition...'

comments

1. There may be occasions when you wish to return unsold items – perhaps because they are not selling as well as you had hoped or, unfortunately, because you are not able to pay for them. Few suppliers provide stock on a sale-or-return basis, so a call of this nature

is always difficult to make. Evidently, you do not want to criticise their goods – especially if you wish to continue trading with them – or admit to financial difficulties, however temporary these may be.

2. Probably the best approach in such circumstances is to indicate that you over-ordered some items, and then ask if they will accept these back for credit to your account. This can avoid the awkwardness of stating that their goods are slow sellers and the embarrassment of explaining your financial affairs. Obviously, if your request is rejected, you will have to reconsider the situation – for example, at a later date, you may have to ask for extended credit facilities, as below.

requesting increased credit facilities

'... and we'd obviously like to see your goods well represented in our expansion plans. But to do this, we'd like to increase our credit limit with you.'

'Let me bring your details up... Wait a moment, please... Okay, what did you have in mind, Mr Hines?'

'Well, we've ordered about £1,000 a month from you since we opened the account last year, and have always paid within 14 days – partly to take advantage of the prompt payment discount that you offer, but also because we need to work within the £1,000 credit limit, which is very restricting. We'd like to see this raised to £2,000, to help us with our plans.'

comments

1. Sometimes you will want to increase the credit limit on your account with a supplier – typically, because you

are expanding and need to carry more stock to do this. Always concentrate on such a positive reason when making your request, even if you wish to buy more from that source because of the problems involved in obtaining comparable goods and services from other suppliers (with whom you have limited credit facilities or poor trading relations).

2. If you have been dealing with this supplier for some time, your request will be judged mainly on how you have managed the account so far – the amounts ordered and the regularity of your payments, in particular. Thus, you should concentrate on these areas during the conversation. If you are still a relatively new customer – that is, a year, or less – then you should support your request by offering bank and trade references. Ideally, referees will be reputable and well known to the supplier.

the demand for payment

'Hello, Miss Kipling. This is the Accounts Department at Atwell, Barker & Browning. We're ringing about invoice 121 for £1,947.20, dated 4 June. This was due for payment on 4 July. We sent two reminders out, on 18 July and 2 August, but have not yet received payment. Have you forwarded payment recently?'

'Just a moment, please... no, I haven't done. I'm sorry; it should have been paid by now. I'll write out a cheque for you now and post it to you by first-class post tomorrow morning. You should have it by Friday at the latest.'

comments

1. If you are telephoned by a supplier demanding

payment of an overdue bill or outstanding account, your response should be a standardised one – assuming that you wish to keep trading with them and maintain a good reputation in your trade or industry.

2. Should you have overlooked payment, apologise immediately, promise to make payment by an agreed date and apologise again. Forward the payment on the stated date. Thus, relations should be kept on an amicable footing.
3. If you are experiencing financial difficulties, you should apologise straight away, explain the situation and then come to some arrangement to clear the debt as soon as possible – as described below. Reaching such an agreement, adhering to it, and even paying off the balance sooner if you can, will help to sustain your relationship with that supplier.

asking for extended credit facilities, accepted

'Hello, Malcolm. It's Terry at RTZ Products. We've just taken delivery of parts from you, and to be honest, I think we may have a problem paying the bill at the usual time. I'm sorry about this, but can we come to some arrangement?'

'What's the problem?'

'Well, as you'll know, one of our customers, Wellmans, has just closed down unexpectedly, and it's no secret that they owe us money. Obviously, we're sorting this out as fast as we can, but it's causing us temporary difficulties.'

'Okay, what did you have in mind?'

'I'd like to suggest paying in three instalments on this occasion. I can let you have the first cheque straight away, with the other two at the same time next month, and the one after that. If we get our money sooner than expected, we'll obviously settle with you immediately.'

'Assuming this is a one-off, I think I can agree with that. Won't the Wellman closure cause you long-term problems?'

'No, definitely not. I'll tell you why...'

comments

1. Asking to pay a bill late, perhaps by a series of smaller payments, is always an embarrassing call to have to make because it is obvious that you are experiencing financial difficulties, which is a worrying sign for suppliers. However, it is better to make this call and try to come to some arrangement, than to leave it until they contact you or to ignore the problem completely. This is more likely to damage relations with suppliers, perhaps irreparably so.
2. Telephone the supplier as soon as you realise there will be a problem. Identify it, give a brief, believable reason and apologise for the situation. Make an offer, which must include an immediate, first payment to be sent straight away (as a sign of good faith), and a promise that if circumstances change for the better, full settlement will then be made. Ask for their agreement to this offer.
3. If they agree, follow the call with written confirmation and your first payment. Make sure that you can adhere to this agreement to avoid further problems and loss of goodwill. If unexpected problems arise – because of circumstances beyond your control – let the supplier know straight away and try to renegotiate a revised arrangement, rather than be chased for payment, which will then make it more difficult for you to reach an amicable agreement. And if you can

pay earlier than expected, consider doing so. It can improve relations significantly.

asking for extended credit facilities, refused

'No, I'm sorry, Mr Regan, but I can't agree to that at all. We're a small firm, and cannot afford to carry around outstanding debts of this size. If all our customers did this, we'd be out of business.'

I'm very sorry, Miss Rowlands. Can you tell me what would be acceptable to you?'

'I'd like to see the bill paid at the agreed time, in accordance with our standard trading terms. You were supplied with the stock on that basis.'

'I'd like to do that too, but unfortunately I cannot. As I say, Thomsons' unexpected overnight closure has left us temporarily short of funds. We do attach the highest priority to paying this bill at the earliest opportunity and would like to come to an amicable, compromise agreement with you. How about if we pay half now, with the balance in two, equal instalments, next month and the one after. If the situation improves before that, we'll settle immediately.'

'No, I'm still not happy with that. I appreciate the position with Thomsons, although most people were aware that something was wrong and took steps to protect themselves in case this happened. What monies have you got coming in over the next month or two?'

'Our incomings and outgoings are fairly steady, with the obvious exception of Thomsons. In terms of income, we expect to receive...'

comments

1. Sometimes the recipient of your request for extended credit facilities will not agree with your suggestions, as they did on page 72, and you will have to try to negotiate a compromise arrangement. Evidently, this can be embarrassing as you may be asked to prove that you are not able to settle the debt as and when it falls due.
2. In this situation, it is especially important that you are in full possession of the facts and know what your incomings, outgoings and their timings are likely to be. Also, you must decide what (if any) parts of this information you are willing to share with the caller. In general, the more details you give, the more likely it is that you will be able to come to an amicable compromise. However, it is unlikely that you will want them to know too much – for example, that you attach a higher priority to paying other debts. Thus, a careful balance needs to be struck.

4

conversing with employees

In some companies, problems exist between managers and employees, and often these can be attributed to a lack of communication or poor communication methods and techniques. Usually, many of these difficulties can be resolved through better communication, which should be conducted on a face-to-face basis, although there will be occasions when the telephone needs to be used. Telephone conversations of this nature can be classified in various ways:

- those relating to the recruitment and selection of staff;
- those dealing with employees who are off sick, some of whom may wish to discuss work or personal problems;
- those made to or received by members of staff who work some distance away – for example, sales representatives.

the speculative enquiry about a possible job opportunity

'Hello, Mr Waller. My name's Bud Driscoll and I've been selling kitchen equipment in the London area for 20 years now. I'm looking for a new job. Do you have anything available?'

'We're fully staffed at present, Mr Driscoll, but if you'd like to send your curriculum vitae in, marked for the attention of the Personnel Section, they'll keep your information on file and send you details of forthcoming vacancies. Thank you.'

'Have you got a minute, Mr Waller? I'd like to tell you a bit about myself.'

'I'm very busy at the moment, Mr Driscoll, and we really are fully staffed. Do please forward your CV though. Personnel will make a note of your details and keep you posted on developments. Thank you for calling.'

'Who should I contact, then?'

'Just mark the envelope for the attention of the Personnel Section, and one of our team will deal with it. Now if you'll excuse me, Mr Driscoll, I'm very busy. Thank you for your call. Goodbye.'

comments

1. Anyone in a position of authority – and especially those who have the power to hire and fire – will be approached regularly by job hunters on an 'on-spec' basis. Generally, it is advisable to discourage contact by telephone since these calls will come at all hours of the day and many callers will be very persistent. On those occasions when such calls are anticipated – when

news of the firm's planned expansion is announced, for example – it is wise to have someone in place to screen and deal with them. Alternatively, you may wish to use an answering machine for screening purposes.

2. If a caller does get through, politely but firmly outline the current position, invite them to submit their curriculum vitae to whoever is responsible for recruitment, and indicate that they will be notified of any vacancies as and when they arise. Thank them for their interest and draw the conversation to a close. As a prospective customer and/or employee, you do want to keep on good terms, but do not wish to be involved in a time-consuming and potentially disruptive conversation. Also, it is important that all applicants are treated exactly the same – in this case, the firm's Personnel Section will deal with them in the first instance.

inviting a job applicant to an interview

'273495.'

'Good morning, can I speak to Andrew Bartlett, please?'

'Speaking.'

'Hello, this is Nancy Williams from ZX Products Limited. You applied for the job of quality control co-ordinator with us and we'd like to invite you to an interview for it. Are you free next Wednesday morning at 11.30?'

'Um, yes... Yes, definitely.'

'Good, can you come to our Head Office at 34–36 Stanley Road, and report to reception at 11.15. They'll then pay your travelling expenses and show you through. The interview will last about half-an-hour and will be conducted by me, Nancy Williams.'

'Yes, yes that's fine. Thank you very much.'

'I'll drop you a line tonight just to confirm the arrangements. Do you know where our Head Office is?'

'Sort of. It's near the station, isn't it?'

'Fairly near. I'll enclose a map for you and highlight the station and our premises on it.'

comments

1. Some companies arrange to conduct selection interviews on one particular morning, afternoon or day, notify successful job applicants in writing and then discount those who do not attend at that time. Such an approach is understandable if panel interviews are being held and interviewers' schedules have to be co-ordinated carefully, but it does not increase their prospects of recruiting the right person for the job. The ideal candidate may not be able to come along at the specified time. Whenever possible, it is advisable to telephone to arrange a mutually agreeable date and time (and place).
2. Various points need to be put across during this call – in particular, the date, time, place and length of the interview and who will be conducting it. You may also want to ask them to bring with them work samples, proof of their qualifications or other materials. It can be helpful to say what they should do on arrival, especially if travel expenses are to be reimbursed at that stage. You may wish to check that they have noted the date, time and place of the interview if they seem nervous and uncertain, or live some distance away.

3. Always follow up a telephone call of this nature with a letter confirming the key points again – it is surprising how many people do not remember what you told them, and need to ring back to verify some of the information. Enclose a map with the location of your firm, and the nearest car park and railway station highlighted upon it. This should help to ensure that those people travelling some distance arrive more easily and on time.

conducting a telephone interview

'... and thinking about that job, Paula, what did you do in an average day?'

'It was a typical receptionist's job in a busy small business, so I did a bit of everything – answering the phone, connecting callers, fielding unwanted calls, taking messages, greeting visitors, showing them to a seat. Of course, we were all expected to muck in and help out at times, so I did my fair share of unloading deliveries, and so on.'

'How did you feel about doing work that was outside the range of your usual duties?'

'Fine. It was a small firm, and there were times when we had to cover for each other and work as a team.'

'Okay... so moving on, what qualities could you bring to this job?...'

comments

1. On occasions, you will wish to conduct preliminary interviews with job applicants over the phone, particularly if the work involves using the telephone – for

example, with telesales. This can be a good way of shortlisting a limited number of candidates who are worth inviting for a face-to-face interview. You can assess their speech and ability to converse (which may be key requirements for this job) and ask direct questions that cannot be avoided, as they might be on an application form.

2. When making a call of this nature, have various documents to hand – a job description, an employee specification (outlining the qualities required of the successful candidate), a list of questions you want to ask and (if relevant) the person's letter of application, curriculum vitae or application form.
3. Ask 'open' questions – 'how?', 'what?', 'why?' – which encourage the applicant to talk about themselves, their background, strengths, weaknesses, suitability for this job, and their ambitions. Your questions should be designed to produce answers that will enable you to compare the applicant's attributes with the requirements listed on the employee specification.
4. If it is relevant, also be ready to question the applicant about any omissions, anomalies or apparent contradictions in their letter of application, curriculum vitae or application form. Make these questions blunt and direct so that they have to be answered, and clearly – for example, 'I see you did not answer question five. Tell me, have you held a full UK driving licence for five years?'
5. Whether the applicant's performance is good enough to warrant an invitation to a face-to-face interview or suggests that they are not well matched to this particular job, the best way of concluding the conversation is to say that you will be in touch shortly once all the applications have been received and considered. When recruiting, it is essential that everyone is treated fairly and equally. After the closing date for applications,

you can then decide who to call in for interviews, notifying them and rejecting the others, either by telephone or (more easily) by letter.

the enquiry from a job applicant

'Hello, Mr Richards. My name's Robert Turner and I've just applied for the job of Despatch Manager. I wonder if you can tell me how my application is progressing?'

'Unfortunately not. Applications are still being processed and we'll be writing to everyone in due course.'

'Have you read my letter?'

'As I say, we're in the process of dealing with applications and will be in touch once that process has been completed.'

'When do you expect to let people know what's happening?'

'As soon as all the applications have been processed, we'll be writing to everyone. Thank you for your call, Mr Turner. We'll be in touch. Goodbye.'

'Goodbye.'

comments

1. More and more job applicants follow up the submission of a letter, CV or application form with a phone call enquiring about their prospects. The longer the time between acknowledging applications and responding to them, the more calls will be made to you.
2. It is sensible to have someone available to screen and manage these calls on your behalf, but occasionally one or two will reach you. These need to be handled

courteously so that you remain on reasonable terms with the callers, but firmly to discourage further conversation and debate. Job applicants who make these calls will be very persistent if they are given the opportunity.

3. By far the best response in this situation is simply to state that applications are being dealt with and applicants will be contacted soon and at the same time (it is good practice to notify everyone simultaneously). Specifying an approximate date can help to satisfy the applicant and terminate the conversation more easily, but only provide this information if you are certain that it is realistic. If it is not, you may be inundated with more and increasingly aggressive calls shortly afterwards.
4. Be prepared to repeat the same comment, albeit in slightly varied ways, if the caller persists. It is important that you do not open up and allow a time-consuming conversation to develop, with the caller trying to sell themselves and to persuade you to grant them an interview. You must be ready to draw the call to a close as soon as possible, politely but very firmly indeed.

asking for a reference

'Jenny Taylor.'

'Hello, Miss Taylor. My name is Tom Cooke. I'm the Human Resources Manager at Grant-Williams. We've received an application from a Lucy Spendlove for the post of Clerical Assistant in our Administration Department, and she has given us your name as a referee. Do you have a few minutes to discuss this application?'

'Yes, I've been expecting your call. What would you like to know?'

'Well, first let me tell you about the job that Lucy has applied for. She'd be responsible for answering the phone, sorting and distributing mail, some word processing and photocopying. General administrative duties, really. What did she do for you?'

'Much the same thing, I'd say. She did a good job. Very reliable person.'

'How long did she work for you?'

'Oh, two years, maybe a bit more. She left in October.'

'Why was that?'

'Personal reasons. Her family was moving North and she wanted to go with them.'

'Would you have her back?'

'In theory, yes. She was a good worker. Obviously, she's been replaced now, though, so there isn't a vacancy.'

'There are a few areas I want to look at in particular – time-keeping, conduct, ability and honesty. What can you tell me about her time-keeping?'

'It was fine, as far as I can remember. I certainly don't recall any problems at all.'

'And her conduct? What was that like?'

comments

1. References are normally taken up either after an interview but before a job offer or, when the referee is a current employer, following an offer of employment that may be subject to the receipt of satisfactory

references. It is advisable to insist on a reference from the present employer, rather than accept the names of other people who may be the applicant's friends or even relatives. It is not unknown for some applicants to give (divorced) parent's (new) names for reference purposes. Written references are often bland and non-committal (for legal reasons), so telephone whenever possible to obtain more off-the-record comments.

2. Always start by telling the referee about the job so that they can comment on the applicant's suitability for it. Ask how long the applicant was employed by the referee and in what capacity. Then raise questions about the applicant's ability, conduct, time-keeping, and honesty – for example, 'What can you tell me about…?' and 'What were they like with regard to…?' Check on the reasons for leaving to see if these match what you have been told. Ask if the referee would re-employ them, too. This will often produce a revealing answer.

making a job offer, accepted

'Good morning. Can I speak to Danny Flowers, please?'

'Yes, that's me.'

'Hello, Danny. This is Petra Chivers at the IPFA. I'm telephoning to offer you the post of Library Assistant at our Head Office. Would you like the job?'

'Oh, yes… yes, that's terrific. Thank you.'

'Do you have a few minutes?'

'Yes, I do.'

'Good. I'd like to go through the main terms of employment with you. First, your salary... Do you have any questions about these terms and conditions, Danny?'

'No, they're all very clear.'

'Fine. I'll be putting everything in writing to you later on today. You can always come back to me after you've read the letter, if you think of anything... Now, I need your permission to contact your present employer, Ted Buxton. As I've said, this offer is subject to a satisfactory reference. Can I telephone him to speed things up?'

'Yes, no problem. His number's 277031, extension 22.'

'Okay, I'll call him later on. Finally, we need to agree on a starting date. I was thinking of...'

comments

1. You can make a job offer to a successful candidate over the telephone or in writing. Often, it is best to phone initially to see if they will accept and, if so, to discuss terms and conditions, and to sort out reference details and starting dates. This conversation can then be followed by a letter confirming what was said and agreed.
2. Begin by making the offer of employment. Hopefully, this will be accepted by the candidate, and often with delight, especially if they have been unemployed for some time.
3. Summarise the main terms and conditions of employment – salary, hours of work, holidays, and so on. Ideally, all the key points will have been covered in any advertisements, in documents sent out with application forms and at the interview. Refer to any that may have been omitted, and ask the candidate if they have any queries about them. State that further details will be put in writing.
4. Ask for permission to take up references – ideally from current and/or most recent employers, and preferably over the telephone to increase your chances of being

given accurate and honest, off-the-record information. Also, agree a starting date, which should be mutually convenient to both parties.

5. Always follow the telephone conversation with a letter confirming all of the main points discussed, just in case anything is forgotten or overlooked. As appropriate, enclose any contractual documents and supporting materials such as the company's staff handbook in which terms and conditions of employment are listed and explained in detail.

making a job offer, rejected

'Good afternoon. Is that Raj Patel?'

'Yes, it is.'

'Hallo, Raj. This is Gary Urdzik from the Thomas Motor Company. Following last week's meeting, I'd like to offer you the job of Works Manager at our Hollingston plant.'

'Thank you... but I'm afraid to say that I'll not be accepting your kind offer.'

'I see. Well, we were very impressed with your application, Raj, and by what you had to say at the interview. We feel you are ideally suited to the job, and thought it seemed the right one for you. May I ask why you're turning it down?'

'I'm not sure, really. I'm not certain if it's right for me, I suppose.'

'Will you be staying at Ransomes, then?'

'For the moment, yes.'

'Raj, tell me what that job offers that ours doesn't.'

'To be honest, the pay package is a bit better...'

'Okay, well we can talk about that...'

comments

1. Occasionally, an offer of employment will be rejected by your preferred candidate. If this is unexpected – perhaps because it has never happened to you before – your immediate response may be one of incredulity and even anger. Clearly, this is not helpful, as it will simply create an unpleasant, confrontational atmosphere from which no one will benefit. It is far better to remain calm and polite so that you can discover the reasons for rejection, and then proceed from there.
2. Sounding friendly, ask them why they are rejecting your offer – maybe they have decided they are happy in their existing post, learned something about your job at the interview that made them change their mind, or have received a better offer from elsewhere.
3. If they are staying where they are or have accepted another offer, ask them how that job compares with the one you are offering them. Typically, they will comment on the pay, fringe benefits or something else. If you want to recruit this person, you may then decide to try to negotiate agreeable terms with them. You will probably have to match or even improve upon the other offer.
4. Should they mention a negative feature of your company, department or position as the cause of rejection – and some people will try to be diplomatic – you may feel that it would not be worthwhile to try to persuade them to change their mind. However, it will enable you to identify company shortcomings and weaknesses, and thus to benefit indirectly from this difficult conversation. These failings, which may well be offputting to other candidates too, can then be addressed and remedied.

the enquiry from a job applicant

'Peter? Is that Peter?'

'Speaking.'

'Oh, hi Peter. It's Perry Martin. You interviewed me for the researcher's post on Monday. How are you doing?'

'I'm well, but very busy.'

'I won't take up much of your time. I just wanted to know how you were getting along with sorting out the applications.'

'We're dealing with them now and will be in touch next week, as promised.'

'Yes, I know. I thought I'd just ring for a progress report. Have you reached a decision yet?'

'We're still considering them and will let everyone know next week.'

'How have I done?'

'As I say, we're still dealing with the applications and will let everyone know our decision at the same time. I can't add anything to that at the moment, Perry. Now if you'll excuse me, I'm very busy. We'll be in touch next week. Thank you.'

comments

1. In many ways, this is a comparable call to the one from a job applicant on page 82. Potentially, it is more difficult though. Someone who has been interviewed will feel that they are that much closer to a job offer and might be more insistent, even desperate for some news, especially if they have been waiting for some time. (It is therefore sensible to indicate at the

interview when they will be contacted, but make sure that you can keep to this deadline.) Also, you may have established a rapport with them at their interview and could now feel obliged to talk to them. Your approach should be the same as before, though – polite but firm.

2. State that the applications are still being considered and that you will contact everyone at a specified time (as referred to at the interview). As before, you may need to repeat this comment in a variety of ways. Be careful not to allow a conversation to develop that may become awkward and embarrassing, and eventually even abusive if the caller suspects that they are not going to be selected. Draw the call to a close if necessary, if they are not prepared to take 'no' for an answer.

the notification of sickness

'Hello, Mr Castle, this is Eddie Andrews from the Advertising Department.'

'Morning, Eddie. How can I help you?'

'I'm just telephoning to say I'll not be at work today as I'm not well.'

'Oh, I'm sorry to hear that, Eddie. What's the matter?'

'I feel awful. It's flu, I think. I've got a rotten headache and a cough. I ache a bit as well. I hope I'll feel better in a day or two.'

'Well, make sure you're feeling better before coming back to work. Is there anything we can do for you at all?'

'Could you tell Eileen to look after the Mashaw file for me? It's on my desk and really needs to be dealt with in the next couple of days.'

'Yes, I'll do that. Now, you're aware of company policy on sickness because we covered it in training the week before last. You can self-certify for five days and then need a doctor's certificate.'

'Yes, I'm familiar with that. I'm sure I'll be back by Thursday – Friday at the latest.'

'Okay. I'll make a note of your call and what's wrong, and that you expect to be back by Friday. We'll give you a call before then, to see how you're progressing. Meantime, look after yourself, and concentrate on getting yourself better...'

comments

1. On (hopefully rare) occasions, some members of staff try to pass off unauthorised absence as a period of illness. Consequently, some managers sometimes tend to assume that anyone who phones in sick falls into this category. Avoid jumping to this conclusion, since it will inevitably create ill feeling between you and the caller. Many people are off sick for relatively short periods due to colds and flu, and the majority of them make considerable efforts to return to work as soon as possible. Whatever your doubts, treat them fairly and with respect.
2. Thus, your approach to this incoming call should be friendly and concerned. Commiserate with them, asking them how they are or what is wrong and whether there is anything you or the firm can do to help. Advise them on company policy and procedures with regard to sickness, self-certification and when a doctor's certificate is required. Obtain any information you need for the completion of company forms. Ask them when they are likely to return so that you can arrange cover for them, if appropriate, and offer your sympathies again. Indicate that you will keep in touch (see below).

calling an absent employee

'Gaz? It's Penny Wellbeck. I just wanted to give you a quick call to see how you are, and if there's anything you need at all.'

'I'm still rather groggy at the moment. I've a stomach upset too.'

'Oh dear, I'm sorry to hear that. A stomach upset can be rather nasty. Have you seen a doctor yet? They might be able to give you something to help that you can't get over the counter.'

'Not yet, no. I feel too ill to go.'

'Well, I'm sure they'd come out to you as you're that ill. Or I'll run you in if you like. We live fairly close to each other, after all.'

'Well, I'll see what I can do. I'll give them a ring.'

'That's a good idea. Let me know if you'd like me to give you a lift. I'd be pleased to do so. I'm sure it would help. Also, the company will want a doctor's certificate if you're going to be off sick after Wednesday. Do you think you'll feel better by then?'

'I don't know. I still feel very rough.'

'Well, if you can get to a doctor, they'll be able to help and give you some idea of how long it's likely to last. It would be helpful if you could let me know too, as I need to draw up the duty rotas for next week in the next day or two...'

comments

1. It is sensible to maintain contact with someone who is off sick – typically, by phoning them when their period of self-certification is at an end, and at agreed, regular

intervals thereafter, as appropriate. This call serves several purposes. It shows concern for those who are genuinely unwell, while indicating to those who are not that their absence is being monitored. Also, it enables any work-related and/or personal problems to be raised informally and discussed, as seen on pages 94 and 96.

2. This conversation needs to be handled sensitively so that it is seen as being supportive, rather than as an attempt to either catch them out or hurry them back to work before they are well enough to return. Ask how they are progressing and if there is anything at all that you or the business can do for them. Remind them gently of company policy and procedures, and ask them for any information you need to complete documentation. Try to discover when they expect to return, stressing that you need this information so that you can arrange the necessary cover during their absence. Be sympathetic throughout the conversation.
3. When an employee comes back to work after a lengthy period of sickness, it is helpful to arrange an interview with them to discuss how they are, what was wrong with them and if they have any special needs that need to be catered for (perhaps temporarily) as a result of their sickness. Again, this conveys a caring image, helps to identify and (hopefully) overcome potential difficulties, and ease that person back into the day-to-day routine. In addition, it sends a clear signal to existing and prospective malingerers that all absences are monitored and subsequently investigated (albeit diplomatically).

counselling an unhappy employee with work-related problems

'Okay, well I do sympathise with your position in this matter, Adam. But I can see David's viewpoint too, and I know you've been around long enough to do so as well. Imagine you've been made redundant, have been off work for some time, and then get the chance of a new job. How would you feel?'

'Well, I'd be relieved... pleased, I guess.'

'Yes, you'd be really pleased and keen to make your mark, and to impress people. And that's what David is trying to do.'

'He's trying to change everything that's worked perfectly well for ages. And everyone's fed up with it.'

'David's got a lot of experience and expertise in this field. You have, too. You've been here for a long while now. How can we get the best from both of you?'

'I just want him to slow down a bit and listen to me.'

'Have you told him that?'

'...not as such, no. He doesn't really listen.'

'It seems to me it would be a good idea if we all sat down together and talked to each other. What do you think, Adam?'

comments

1. Sometimes, employees will raise work-related problems over the telephone rather than on a face-to-face basis or in writing. Difficulties with colleagues, new working practices, an increased workload or whatever,

can seem less embarrassing to talk about at a distance. Follow a set of guidelines when handling a conversation of this nature.

2. Try to discover what the problem is. This may not be obviously apparent. Find out its cause and all the facts of the matter. Be prepared to give the employee plenty of time to speak, and encourage them to talk by sounding concerned and non-judgemental – for example, by saying 'Mmm', 'Go on', or 'Tell me more'. Distinguish between facts and opinions. This is not easy to do, especially if the person is emotional.
3. It can be useful to repeat their comments, perhaps in a more coherent and logical manner, to check that you have understood all the main points, and that this is what they meant to say. At this stage, you may wish to draw the conversation to a close, promising to look into the matter, and return the call at an agreed time. Alternatively, you may feel that you know enough to deal with it now, typically discussing the matter and encouraging them to see not only their viewpoint, but others' too.
4. It is often sensible to attempt to work towards a mutually satisfactory solution to the problem; the more involved the disgruntled employee is with this process, the better. Alternatively, it may be possible to refer the matter to a third party, to arbitrate or advise accordingly. It is often tempting to try to resolve problems straight away and to do it yourself, when it might be wiser to acknowledge that this is a serious problem that requires greater and more experienced attention than can be provided by you in a phone call.
5. You may wish to follow this conversation by making a written note of its contents for future reference, and/or passing the matter on to someone who is more suited to resolving the situation. It is important that you do not try to handle matters beyond your areas of activity and expertise.

counselling an unhappy employee with personal difficulties

'I'm really sorry to hear about this, Victoria, and do sympathise with the position you're in. It's obviously very difficult for you.'

'I just don't know what to do about it…'

'Sometimes, it can help if some sort of independent expert looks at the problem. Have you thought of approaching someone for advice?'

'No, not really. I don't know what to do. That's why I'm asking you.'

'Well, I'd certainly like to help you, but I really don't know enough to advise you properly. How about contacting the Citizens' Advice Bureau in Crescent Road, behind the library? They'd know more about this than me, and will certainly have some names and numbers of people who can give you the specialist assistance you need…'

comments

1. As with the previous conversation on page 94, some members of staff will want to talk about their personal difficulties on the telephone, perhaps after they have been off sick for a period of time as a consequence of them. Clearly, dealing with such issues as financial pressures, the breakdown of a relationship and the like, requires great tact and diplomacy, and often professional expertise that you don't have the time or ability to provide personally. Hence, you need to approach a conversation of this kind with extreme care.

2. Unless you are trained and experienced in handling an employee's personal problems, probably the best approach is to be sympathetic and willing to listen, while encouraging that person to seek independent, professional help – for example from a debt counsellor at a Citizens' Advice Bureau, a doctor, or whoever is appropriate. Always try to supply a name, contact number, and so on, by way of encouragement. This shows that you're taking the matter seriously, and are trying to help.
3. Follow up this conversation by making a note of what was said and agreed, and passing on this information, in line with company policies and procedures. Typically, you might make a note of this on file. And you may wish to memo your line manager (if appropriate) so that it's all recorded properly. The key point here is to be supportive, but to leave counselling of an intimate and personal nature to those who are qualified to provide it.

thanking a colleague

'Sylvia Buchanan'.

'Sylvia? It's John. John Jones. I just wanted to give you a quick call to thank you for looking over that contract for me.'

'Oh, that's my pleasure, John. I was pleased to do it.'

'I'm very grateful, though, Sylvia. To be honest, I wasn't familiar with some of the areas, so your advice was invaluable. I know it must have taken up quite a bit of your time and I appreciate it. Thank you.'

'My pleasure...'

comments

1. Too often in business, acts of generosity and kindness above and beyond normal working courtesies are taken for granted, making it far less likely that they will be repeated in the future. A simple 'thank you' should suffice, although a handwritten note and perhaps a small gift (chocolates, flowers, wine) may be more appropriate on those occasions when someone has been especially kind.
2. Say why you are calling, how they have helped you and then pay them a brief compliment – perhaps referring to their expertise or the time they have spent assisting you. Conclude by saying thank you. Often, such a simple phrase will have a much greater impact than extensive, and what may appear to be insincere, expressions of gratitude. Phone exclusively to thank them, rather than mentioning it in passing in another call. Again, this has more impact.

praising an employee

'Derek Walker.'

'Hi, Derek. It's Paul Kingston at Head Office. How are you?'

'I'm well, thank you. And yourself?'

'I'm fine. I'm calling to thank you for handling the Trenton situation for the company. You did a great job.'

'Well, thank you. Thanks very much. I was pleased to do it.'

'I thought it was one of those occasions that required considerable tact and diplomacy if we were going to retain their business. To be frank, I expected to lose the contract, but I think your persuasive skills won them over. In fact, I would not be surprised if they increased their order. It's down to you Derek, and we're really grateful. Thank you.'

comments

1. In many ways, this is a similar phone call to the one thanking a colleague on page 97. However, it is generally best to thank someone of a similar standing to you rather than praise their qualities as this can seem to be patronising. It is always sensible to praise employees as and when appropriate, though, since this acts as a motivator.
2. Make this call a simple one for maximum impact. State why you are phoning, acknowledge whatever it is that they have done and praise them for it. Add a phrase like 'well done' to end the call. Phone just to praise them, rather than dealing with other issues too, which may detract from the praise. If the employee's activities have been particularly impressive, it may be a good idea to put your comments in writing so that they are kept on file and seen during subsequent appraisals.

encouraging an employee to improve

'Jessica Barton.'

'Hello, Jessica. It's Ian Matthews. How are you?'

'Very well, thank you. And yourself?'

'I'm well, too. I'm ringing all our agents this evening to talk to them about our sales. You know we've always been impressed by what you do for us, but sales have really been dropping for some time now and we want to see how we can reverse this trend. Do you have any ideas why they're falling?'

'Difficult to say for sure... um, I think it's probably a combination of things. Some independents have closed and others are on the edge. Hasketts has been very active in the area lately. And, of course, it is that time of year when sales are traditionally low. I'm sure things will pick up in the summer.'

'I agree with what you say, Jessica, although there may be other factors involved too, which we need to address. Concentrating on what you've said, what can we do – you and me – to improve matters?'

'Well, to start with, I'd like to see the company co-ordinate its sales and production a lot better. I lose sales because I can't guarantee deliveries. Even when customers do order, the goods are often so late that they're angry and reluctant to reorder.'

'That's a good point. What about your side, Jessica? What can you do to help us?'

'Hard to say. I suppose I could call on them more often, but I'm not sure if that would help much, and it would be difficult to organise...'

'That's an excellent thought. I think it's one that's worth developing. Let me suggest something to you...'

comments

1. Encouraging an employee to work harder and better is always tricky to do over the telephone, but it may be necessary on occasions – for example when you are dealing with sales agents. It becomes even more difficult when they are unaware that they need to improve and are complacent about the existing situation.

2. To begin with, you should identify the problem, calmly and in a matter-of-fact way without apportioning blame. It is usually best if the employee can be encouraged to identify their own shortcomings, as this is less confrontational and tends to produce better results.
3. Next, ask them for their comments. Give them time to gather their thoughts if you can, or accept that their initial comments may be incomplete and illogical. Be prepared to extend the conversation and repeat the same question in different ways if necessary, to obtain a full and accurate picture.
4. Then put across your views, although you will need to do this diplomatically and in a positive way if you are to encourage rather than demoralise them. Obviously, this is easier to do if the employee has identified some key areas of concern, which you can then look at in more detail.
5. Always ask what 'we' can do to improve matters, rather than what 'you' are going to do (even if the employee is wholly at fault). Various company failings may be highlighted by the employee's comments. Also, such a non-confrontational question should encourage them to focus on their own weaknesses, albeit perhaps superficially at first.
6. Be ready to encourage them to keep talking until they refer to those areas of greatest concern to you. These can then be considered more closely. Keep trying to get the employee to recognise what they are doing wrong and how they can resolve their shortcomings. Say what you will do to help them, follow this through and speak again later at an agreed date to monitor progress so far.

disciplining an employee

'Morning David, it's Nina Givens. How are you?'

'I'm okay. What can I do for you?'

'Well, there's a problem, David, and I'm ringing you because we may not get the chance to speak on our own at tomorrow's busy meeting, and I don't want to formalise this by putting it in writing.'

'... Sounds rather ominous.'

'It shouldn't be, David. Not if we can get it sorted out now. When we took you on, you agreed to call on the 50 key accounts in your territory once a month, and the rest at least once every two months. I've received calls from four of our main customers commenting that you're not visiting as often as that. Looking at the sales orders you've submitted lately, that seems to be a common problem. Can you tell me what's happening?'

'Well, I found that I wasn't getting orders from some customers every month, so I call less frequently and use the extra time to chase new custom. As you know, I've opened five new accounts recently.'

'Yes, that's something else I wanted to raise with you. I'll come to that in a minute. As far as our existing customers are concerned, we wouldn't expect you to obtain orders from all of them every month, but they do need to be visited – to update them, answer their queries and be seen. Just be there to reassure them, and keep them happy. Otherwise, they'll drift away, especially if someone else comes on the scene.'

'What about new customers? Aren't they worth pursuing?'

'I'd rather you concentrated on the existing accounts at this time and maintained their sales. We can discuss other opportunities once this problem has been remedied. Can you start monthly visits from the beginning of next month?'

'Yes, I can do that. Do you have any other problems with my work?'

'No, not at all. The other feedback I'm getting is very positive. You're friendly and personable, and the customers like you. They'd just like to see you more often! Will you make sure they do from now on?'

'Yes, I will...'

'Okay, well, let's talk again next month to see how we're getting along...'

comments

1. The disciplining of any employee should always adhere closely to company and legal guidelines – typically, comprising two verbal warnings followed by two written warnings and ultimately dismissal if the employee's work performance and/or conduct does not improve, despite these warnings, opportunities to remedy shortcomings and assistance to do so.
2. Disciplining someone over the telephone is usually inappropriate, although there may be occasions when you want to deal with a problem in an informal, off-the-record manner, before formal disciplinary procedures are introduced. Hopefully, such a call may avert the necessity of on-the-record actions. You should approach this conversation in a set way.
3. Begin by identifying the problem to the employee and explaining its consequences on fellow members of staff, the firm, sales or whatever. If it is relevant, refer to previous conversations on the same subject and how improvements have not been made. Do this in a calm, matter-of-fact way, to avoid the development of a confrontation.

4. All disciplinary procedures must be conducted in a fair and reasonable manner, and this conversation should follow this rule. So give the employee the chance to answer and put their point of view, which you should listen and respond to, questioning them in a courteous way and encouraging them to explain themselves fully and clearly. Give them the benefit of the doubt at this early stage and indicate what you can do to help them.
5. Try to reach agreement on what is going to be done to resolve the difficulty. You need to make it clear what standards are expected of them and by when, what they must do, how you will assist them (if this is relevant) and when you will speak to them again to discuss progress. As appropriate, indicate that you are always available to offer help and advice, as and when required. End on a bright and positive note – ideally, with both parties in agreement and working towards the same goal.
6. Monitor progress in a discreet manner, giving further assistance as agreed or subsequently requested. Talk again at the stated time. Congratulate them warmly if efforts and improvements have been made, and encourage them if there is still some way to go. If the situation remains much the same, you will need to consider implementing formal disciplinary procedures in line with company policy.

giving a reference about an employee

'293. Malcolm Reid speaking.'

'Hello, Mr Reid. My name is Dawn Baxter from EBS; we're an import agency working down at the docks. We've had an application from one of your trainees, Guy Seabrook, who

wants to be a runner for us. What can you tell me about him?'

'Guy Seabrook? He's been here since July on one of our training schemes. He works mainly in the warehouse, sorting and packing goods for despatch, doing the paperwork for this, handling returns, and so on. He does one day a week at Ipsworth College, studying for an advanced GNVQ in Business.'

'I see. What's he like, though?'

'I don't know him on a personal level. He's been appraised twice since he's been here and his overall work-rate and performance in relation to this job were rated 'satisfactory or above' on both occasions. His college report estimates that he will pass his course.'

'Do you think we should offer him this job then, or not?'

'I can't really advise you there. Guy's work here has been satisfactory at all times.'

'Would you recommend him, then?'

'Based on what he's done here and at college, I'm happy to confirm that his work-rate and performance for us have always been acceptable.'

comments

1. Providing a reference about an employee appears to be a relatively straightforward exercise, especially over the phone where you can talk informally and off-the-record. However, it is a difficult call – if you praise the employee and they subsequently prove unacceptable or if you criticise them and they consequently lose their job, then this may have repercussions on you. Often, it is best to supply only written references, whenever possible.

2. If you are telephoned and asked for a reference, the wisest course of action is to adhere to the facts, rather than opinions. Thus, the caller has to reach their own unbiased conclusions and the employee has less cause for complaint than if you expressed your personal feelings. Facts cannot be disputed; opinions can.
3. It can be wise to follow up a telephone conversation of this nature with a letter confirming what you have said. Again, give undisputed facts, rather than arguable opinions. Let the other person decide for themselves how to interpret those facts.

5

handling personal calls

Occasionally, you will have to make, or might receive, personal calls during working hours. Some of these will be of an embarrassing or difficult nature. They can be divided into two main types:

- those made on behalf of yourself – typically, when seeking new employment at another organisation;
- those made or received when representing the firm, on a range of subjects as diverse as asking for a meeting to sympathising with someone on the death of their partner.

enquiring about prospective job opportunities, known contact

'Hallo, Sally. It's Paulo Matteo. How are you?'

'I'm very well, Paulo. And yourself?'

'I'm fine. I'm calling because I'm looking to take on some additional work in the coming year, and wondered if APX is using freelance writers at the moment.'

'No, I'm afraid not. There have been big changes here since you last worked for us. We've been cutting back; everything's now being done in-house. Nothing is sent out.'

'Fair enough. Do you know of any companies in your industry that are still employing freelances to put together their advertising and PR material? Bensons, perhaps?'

'Not that I can think of. Bensons do the same as us – it all comes down to money, doesn't it? Do whatever's the cheapest... mind you, I've a feeling Hans Schugardt at BWZ uses freelances now and then, and possibly Serena Lloyd at Barlays. Do you want me to mention you to them?'

'Yes, please. Perhaps you could let them know I worked as a copywriter at Amacam for eight years, before going freelance three years ago. I produce all types of business advertising copy, but specialise in direct mailings. I won the DMAC award for Consumer Advertising Copy last year.'

'Got it. I'll let them know you're available, Paulo.'

'I'll send you my CV and some work samples for you to pass on. Can you do that this week, if I get them to you in the morning?'

comments

1. One of the most productive ways of finding out about job opportunities is to approach your network of contacts – friends, relatives, former colleagues, current business associates and anyone who may be able either to offer you a position, or to put you in touch with other would-be employers. During a call of this nature, you should aim to cover various key topics.

2. Start by introducing yourself and explaining why you are calling – to enquire about current and/or possible job opportunities at that firm, or elsewhere. Be very clear about the reason for your call – too many people are too circumspect here! This causes confusion.
3. State what type of job you are seeking and, if appropriate, in what sort of company, trade or industry. The more specific you are, the easier it is for the other person to think of suitable possibilities.
4. Say what you have to offer – outlining briefly those strengths that are most closely related to a job, company, trade or industry of this kind. These should refresh the memory and provide some key facts to pass on, if appropriate. Keep it brief though. They'll not remember a long list of points. Choose your best ones to put across.
5. Conclude by asking them to do what you want – for example to grant you an interview, circulate your details to other would-be employers, supply you with their names, addresses and telephone numbers, or to keep you informed of any developments. Make it as easy as possible for them to agree with this – for example, by indicating that you are available to see them at their office, or offering to e-mail or fax through copies of your curriculum vitae, and so on.

enquiring about prospective job opportunities, unknown contact

'Give me two minutes, Mrs Hunt, to tell you about myself, and what I can do for you... I was the human resources manager at Johnson White for nine years, until it was taken over and closed down by Boulle last year. Since then, I've worked as a freelance consultant producing stress management programmes for organisations such as Devlin & Co, Smyths and Waynes. After these programmes had been implemented, productivity levels increased by more than 5 per cent. Let me tell you what sort of programme I could do for you...'

comments

1. In many ways, this is a comparable call to the one made to a known contact (see page 107), although your approach here may perhaps need to be more formal as you do not know the recipient of your call.
2. Aim to cover the same topics as in the previous conversation – a brief introduction, an explanation of the type of work you are seeking, a description of what you have to offer and a request to meet them or whatever, as appropriate.
3. The main difficulty with this type of call is that you are unknown to the other person, so you will have to work hard and fast to overcome their apathy, or even resistance, if they receive numerous speculative calls like this. Concentrate in particular on what you have to offer and can do for them. Sell yourself as a product or service, as shown on pages 17 and 24.

the invitation to an interview

'Good morning, this is Samantha O'Donnell at Meadow Research. You applied to us for a job as a market researcher. Can you come for an interview next Wednesday at 11 o'clock?'

'The 23rd? Yes, thank you. Where is it being held?'

'We're running interviews at the Waverley Hotel in Wilby Road, Danchester. Do you know it?'

'Yes, I do. It's directly opposite the railway station. Whereabouts in the hotel are you working?'

'I'm not sure just yet. If you go to reception on arrival, they'll show you through to wherever we are.'

'No problem. Can you tell me who will be interviewing me and the length of the interview?'

'I'm not sure at the moment. Probably... Peter Bell or Mandy Prior who run the Personnel Department. They're running preliminary interviews that will last maybe 20 minutes or so. If you're recalled, you'll then go to see Ab Jorna, who's in charge of Research. You'll be with her for about the same length of time, I imagine.'

'Thanks, thanks very much. While you're on, would it be possible for me to obtain some company literature and a job description before the interview? I'd be happy to come in to collect these if you could perhaps leave them in reception for me.'

'I don't see why not. Leave it with me and I'll sort something out this afternoon. You can pick them up from the end of today onwards.'

'Excellent. Thank you. I look forward to reading them and seeing you at the Waverley at 11 o'clock on Wednesday the 23rd...'

comments

1. If you are telephoned and invited to an interview for a job, you should have two aims in mind – to get all the key facts about the interview so that you can arrive on time and well prepared, and to obtain any other information you need about the industry, company, job or person required to enable you to decide if this is the right position for you, and vice versa.

2. With regard to the interview, you must know the date, time and exact location. Also, it is helpful to be aware of where to go and who to ask for on arrival, the names, job titles and roles of the interviewers and the length of the interview. If any of these points are not covered – and it is always unwise to assume that everything will be – be ready to ask for confirmation, as and when relevant.
3. Any extra information you are seeking concerning the industry, company, job and/or the type of person required will depend on what details have already been obtained – for example from documents sent to you with an application form, and from your own desk and field research, and so on. Again, be prepared to ask questions, but be conscious that the caller will probably be busy and will not want to talk at length, so limit the number of questions, and keep them brief and to the point.
4. It is a good idea to follow this conversation with a letter, acknowledging your intention to attend the interview and stating how much you are looking forward to it. This may help to set you apart from the other candidates who will be interviewed also.

the telephone interview

'Tell me a little about your background, Mr Rogers.'

'I've been a sales agent for Sandersons for five years, selling feeding and sterilising equipment very similar to the goods I'd be dealing with in this job. I also cover the same territory – Essex, Suffolk and Norfolk. I know the area and the customers well, having 128 accounts, and many more contacts...'

'And what qualities can you bring to this job?'

'Extensive, hands on experience of being a sales representative for the goods in this trade and in this particular area. I'm ambitious and hardworking, too. In the past five years, I've built up my client base from 53 to 128 accounts. With your company name and products behind me, I can increase your sales, too. Very briefly, this can be done in two ways...'

comments

1. Sometimes, job advertisements will state that you should apply for a job by phone; clearly, this is especially relevant if the post you are applying for involves extensive use of the telephone. Alternatively, you may be called by a prospective employer who has read your letter of application, curriculum vitae or completed application form and wishes to question you further about it, and your reasons for wanting this position.
2. If you are telephoning them, state your name, why you are calling, what job you are applying for and where you learned of it. This helps to focus their attention as swiftly as possible. Then provide a brief and concise description of yourself, your background and those general strengths that are best associated with this type of job, company, trade or industry.
3. Be prepared to say why you want this job, concentrating on positive reasons and using upbeat expressions – 'an opportunity to progress', 'fulfil potential', and so on. Be ready to explain exactly what you can bring to the post and this company, matching very specific strengths with the attributes that are likely to be considered essential and desirable by the organisation.
4. Always give direct and concise answers to any questions asked. Generally, your replies should comprise a

basic statement followed by further, explanatory details as necessary and an example that links one of your strengths to a key quality needed for the position. If questions focus on what might be considered to be negative issues, such as redundancies and periods of unemployment, still try to concentrate on positive matters – how you learned to budget successfully on a limited income while you were unemployed, to organise your time and energies well, and so on.

5. If possible, end the interview by asking them for what you want and make it easy for them to agree with it. Typically, you might ask if you can come to their office to see them for a face-to-face interview, and say that you are free to attend whenever it is most convenient for them. Don't be too pushy, though, if they indicate that they have other telephone interviews to carry out, after which they will consider all the applications and contact people in due course. This is only fair to the other applicants. Follow the conversation with a letter of thanks, referring again to your suitability and enclosing a CV, as appropriate.

the offer of employment, positive response

'Angela Hardacre.'

'Hello, Angela. This is Colette Baker at ABC Windows and Doors. We met last week to discuss the sales processor's job. Are you still interested?'

'Yes, I am, definitely.'

'Good – in that case, we'd like to offer the job to you.'

'Oh, that's excellent news. I'm really pleased to accept.'

'I think we discussed the terms and conditions at our meeting. I just need to ask your permission to approach your employer for a reference. Obviously, our offer is subject to a satisfactory reference, but I'm sure that won't be a problem. Also, I'd like to know when you can start work.'

'Can you just confirm the position regarding working hours? You'll recall I'd like to work 8.30 to 4.30 because I'll be commuting from Werbick. You said you'd check on that for me.'

'Yes, I have, and that's fine. The boss is happy for you to do that.'

'That's great. My line manager here is Ruth Madlow – M-a-d-l-o-w. She's on extension 98 and will be pleased to talk to you about me. She's out this morning, but will be in this afternoon from 2.30 onwards.'

'I'll give her a call later on, then. If all is well, when can you start work for us?'

'I'm supposed to give one week's notice, which should be okay, but I wouldn't want to leave until the company had sorted out some cover for me. Perhaps you can discuss that with Mrs Madlow this afternoon. I'm obviously looking forward to moving.'

comments

1. You may receive a job offer by telephone or in writing. Typically, the initial approach will be made over the phone so that the caller can learn immediately your response and, if favourable, ask for your permission to contact referees and check when you can start work (assuming satisfactory references are received). This will usually be followed by written confirmation and fuller details of the offer of employment.

2. Make a point of requesting verification of any terms and conditions that were not covered (clearly) in the advertisement, in subsequent correspondence or at the interview – you need to know all about these before you start work. Double-check on vague assurances and promises that were made at your interview – these are sometimes forgotten shortly after they have been made.
3. You will be expected to give your present (or most recent) employer as a referee since they will know you best and be able to provide the most valid reference. If you know they will speak favourably of you, encourage the caller to phone them. Their off-the-record comments are likely to be more enthusiastic than a written statement which may be rather bland and circumspect (for legal purposes). Let the referee know that a request for a reference is about to be made.
4. Your suggested date for starting work should take account of your contractual obligations to your existing employer. It is also a good idea to indicate that you do not want to leave until a replacement has been found for you or cover provided by existing staff – assuming, of course, that this will not take too long. Convey the (hopefully accurate) impression that you are a decent and considerate person – the type they want to employ.
5. Always follow a conversation of this nature with a letter confirming your acceptance of the offer, details of terms and conditions agreed (in case of subsequent disputes), permission to approach your referees and the proposed date for the commencement of employment. This is really to ensure that any promises made during the discussion are kept, rather than overlooked, as sometimes happens.

the offer of employment, negative response

'Good morning, may I speak to Cathy Whitmore, please?'

'Speaking.'

'Hi, Cathy. It's Robert Entwhistle at Baxters. I'm ringing to offer you the post of sales adviser in our new clothing department. Can you start Monday week?'

'Hello, Mr Entwhistle... I'm flattered to receive your offer but, to be honest, I don't wish to accept it. I don't feel it's the right move for me. Thank you, though. I am flattered.'

'... Oh... I see... well, if you don't want it, fine. I'll get someone else. Why did you come to the interview, then, if you didn't want the job?'

'I was impressed by what I saw at the interview and think the department and company are excellent, but the job isn't the right one for me. Thank you for the offer, though.'

'What's wrong with the job?'

'It's a good job, but I just don't think it's the one for me, and vice versa.'

comments

1. On rare occasions, you will be offered a job that you do not wish to accept – perhaps you have had second thoughts and prefer to stay where you are, have learned something negative about the job or company at the interview or received a better offer elsewhere. Whatever your reason, this type of call is invariably an awkward and embarrassing one that needs to be handled diplomatically.

2. It is usually best to give a bland, uncritical reason for rejecting the offer so that you can remain on good terms with the caller. A comment along the lines that the job is not right for you – and, by implication, that you are not quite right for the job either – is often most appropriate. Avoid direct criticism of the job and indirect criticism by not mentioning the attributes of your existing job, or another one that you have accepted. Always bear in mind that your paths may cross again some day. So keep on amicable terms.

asking for a meeting

'Yvonne Marven'.

'Hello, Yvonne, this is Freddie Walton. We met at the trade fair last weekend. How are you?'

'I'm well, but rather busy at the moment.'

'I'll not keep you. I'm just ringing to arrange a meeting to see if we can do business together.'

'Oh, well... I'm not sure.'

'We're introducing a number of new lines shortly that would enable you to increase your stock range considerably. They're very competitively priced. You'll be able to compete against the multiples and make a good profit. When are you free next week?'

'I think next week's rather full, if I remember...'

'I'm in Llangolleth on Tuesday, Wednesday, Thursday and Friday, and can come to see you at any time on any of those days. Do you have ten minutes free?'

'All right, hold on. Let me get my diary...'

comments

1. The key to a successful request for a meeting at which you can sell your goods and services, is to make it easy for the other person to say 'yes' and difficult for them to say 'no'. There are various ways of doing this.
2. Make it easy by asking outright for a meeting – there is nothing to be gained by being circumspect here. Give them a good ('what's in it for me') reason why they should meet you, referring to how the products and services will benefit them. Tell them enough to arouse their curiosity and to make them interested to know more, but not so much that their questions are answered immediately – if that happens, it makes it less likely that they will need to meet you.
3. Make it difficult for them to rebuff you by indicating that you are free to meet whenever it suits them. You can suggest that you will be in their area and are happy to come to them. It all helps. It can also be a good idea to imply that a special offer is currently available, but that this is only for a limited period – this may increase your chances of success.

the request for a meeting, positive response

'What exactly do you want to discuss, Mr Hoyt?'

'We're launching mark two versions of the "Daybreak" and "Siesta" and they're going to be big sellers. I want to show you what improvements we've made and how easy these will make it for you to sell them to your customers.'

'Can't we discuss them over the phone?'

'Well, the improvements relate to the folding mechanism and the removal of the seat cover – they really need to be demonstrated. It'll make it that much easier for you to show your customers in turn.'

'Look, I'm free on Monday at 3.30, if you'd like to call in then. I only have 20 minutes, so it will have to be a quick demonstration. If you can leave me some facts and figures, I'll look at those later and come back to you. I won't be ordering anything on the spot. I've another meeting scheduled at 4.00, so this will have to be a short visit. Is that okay?'

comments

1. Although there may be times when you ask to meet someone, there will be as many occasions when people want to arrange a meeting with you to sell you their goods and services. You may be happy to agree to this request, but you should work through two areas of concern before doing so.
2. Find out as much as possible about what the other person wants and can do for you, so that you can decide whether a meeting is likely to be worthwhile for you or not. If pressed, they may be able to give you all the information you need to make a decision over the phone, thus saving your time later on. Alternatively, they might be able to send you details for you to study at your leisure, rather than be harassed by a pushy salesperson at a meeting.
3. If you are agreeable to a meeting, put some constraints on it, making it clear what will be discussed and how much time you have available for them. It is advisable to indicate that you have another appointment or whatever immediately after this meeting. You must stay in control, especially with a potentially insistent salesperson.

the request for a meeting, negative response

'Mr Payne?'

'Speaking…'

'Hello, Mr Payne. My name's Andy Langford, from WPS. I'm in your area next week and would like to come to see you to demonstrate our new products for the coming season. Can you tell me when you're free?'

'Well, thank you for your interest, Mr Langford, but I'm not free to meet you, I'm afraid. We've been doing business with Brands for some time now and are very satisfied with their goods and services for the time being. Give me a call in six months, though, and perhaps we can talk again then…'

comments

1. Rejecting a request to meet appears simple to do – you just say 'no, thank you'. However, it is often more complicated than that. Typically, you will want to maintain an amicable working relationship with the caller, who may be a prospective future supplier, or someone of considerable influence in your trade or industry. Your relationship is unlikely to be sustained unless you can respond diplomatically to their call.
2. Probably the best way of handling it is to be warm and friendly, but regretful. Thank them for their interest, indicate why you cannot meet them – you already have a well-established arrangement with a reliable supplier, you have no work available to offer them, or whatever – and offer hope for the future, if appropriate. Use phrases like '…at the moment' and '…for the time being'. Perhaps suggest that they contact you again at

some date in the future, when the situation might have changed. Make this an encouraging rejection – not an easy task!

introducing an associate to a third party

'While I'm on the phone Tony, a former colleague of mine, Ken Gilbert, has asked me to introduce him to you.'

'Why? What does he want?'

'Well, he's just set up as a management consultant and is seeking work with companies in your sector.'

'Tell me about him.'

'He worked here as our customer relations manager from 1989 until last October when, as you know, the whole company was restructured and the workforce was rationalised. He took voluntary redundancy and then set up his own consultancy practice.'

'Is he any good?'

'He ran the Customer Relations Department for seven years, managing a team of 12 people and dealing with some 500 customers. He's written various articles and had two books published on customer care. He advised Bryan Horton at Greenbury last year, and was involved on a freelance basis in establishing the customer care centre at Newtons.'

'Does he concentrate purely on customer relations management or does he advise on other areas too?'

'He specialises in customer care, but provides advice on other matters as well.'

'And you can recommend him?'

'Well, he worked here for some time, has written about the subject and has had two major contracts with leading companies in recent months...'

comments

1. Now and then, you will be asked to introduce a person you know to someone else – usually with a view to them doing business together. If you know that person well and respect their abilities, you will probably be happy to do this. Be careful, however, because if you recommend them and they subsequently fall short of expectations, your reputation with that third party may be damaged. It is sensible to adopt a slightly cautious approach in such a situation.
2. The best advice that can be given here is simply to introduce the person concerned and provide a fact-based description of them. When answering questions about them, keep to the facts rather than your opinions of them. Encourage the third party to draw their own conclusions, and want to speak to or meet that person without being forced into it by you through persuasion or a sense of obligation. It is preferable to fall short of outright recommendation, unless you are totally confident in their ability to deliver, and are happy to stand or fall with them.

thanking an associate for an introduction

'Paddy Smith.'

'Paddy. It's Tim Jones at Bresslaws. I just wanted to ring to thank you for introducing me to Sally Peterson at Baker–Wilson.'

'My pleasure. Did it help?'

'Yes, it did; very much so. I've just called Sally and we discussed her future stock requirements. She's invited me in for a chat next Thursday afternoon. So, it's looking good.'

'That's terrific. I'm pleased for you.'

'It's down to you, Paddy. Your introduction made it possible. I'm very grateful. Thank you. I owe you one!'

comments

1. It is always sensible to thank someone who has helped you in a professional capacity – typically, by introducing you to another person with whom you can do business. This is not only courteous but develops and maintains the relationship between you, making it more likely that they will assist you again in the future.
2. Your thanks need not be elaborate or effusive – indeed, the fuller they are, the more insincere they can appear to be. Make it simple – say why you are calling, thank them, add a brief explanation, thank them again and then offer to return the favour, if this seems appropriate. It can be a good idea to make this last comment fairly light and humorous to avoid the impression that this is little more than a mercenary, bartering relationship. Ring just to say thank you rather than mention it in another conversation, which will lessen its impact.
3. On occasions, it may seem more fitting to send them a brief handwritten note with a small gift. Make sure, though, that the gift is a modest one (a bottle of wine or a box of chocolates) so that it is regarded as a token of your thanks and not as a pay-off.

congratulating someone on their promotion

'Mike Lucas.'

'Hello, Mike. It's Janice Greene at Intex. I've just read in *The Trader* that you're becoming head of production at Radcester and wanted to congratulate you. It's a great move, isn't it?'

'Yes, it is. It's a big step up. Josh Hunter is taking early retirement and I've been promoted – big department, lots more responsibility. It's a terrific challenge and I'm looking forward to it.'

'You must have had to beat off a lot of rivals for the job. There must have been many applicants.'

'About 60 or 70 applied, I think. Eight were interviewed, three of us were recalled and then I got it.'

'Sounds impressive. How many people are you going to be in charge of, Mike?'

comments

1. As business is often done on a 'who-you-know' rather than on a 'what-you-know' basis, it is worth spending time working on relationships with people of influence. Congratulating (and thanking) them as and when appropriate can help to achieve this. Only congratulate someone on their new job when it is clearly an upwards promotion rather than a sideways transfer to a similar job with a more impressive job title. In that situation, such a call may not be well received.
2. The simpler the call, the better; the act of calling to congratulate will in itself have a significant effect.

Acknowledge the promotion, congratulate them on it and show interest in the new job by asking one or two fairly bland, non-controversial questions about it. These should be easy to answer and enable the other person to appear clever, talented, and so on. Don't comment on any possible negative aspects of the job – the lengthy journey, the need to relocate their family, the long hours, or whatever. Keep the conversation bright and friendly, and leave a positive, lasting impression on them.

congratulating someone on an award

'264. *John Mortimer.*'

'John? It's Eric Roth at Presthaven. We've just been told you've won the X-cel regional award and wanted to congratulate you on it. What was in your portfolio?'

'Oh, I included the "Adventurer" and "Ranger" materials, and the "Arkesaurus" project, too. That was highly commended.'

'Yes, that was really distinctive, especially the 3-D effect that you achieved with it. It was memorable. As I say, John, congratulations from all of us here at Presthaven. You must be feeling very pleased...'

comments

1. In many respects, this is a comparable call to the congratulatory one made to a person who has just been promoted (see page 125). In particular, it can help to develop working relations and needs to be friendly, informal and relatively brief. It is the act of ringing to congratulate that has the most impact.

2. Congratulate them on winning the award and then either speak highly of it if it is a well-known one or ask them about it if not – this gives them the opportunity to talk about themselves. You could then follow their lead, complimenting them as and when appropriate. Say how much they deserved the award and conclude by congratulating them once more. Sound sincere by keeping your praise in proportion to the importance of the award. If you praise them too much, either because you want them to do you a favour at some stage or because you were a runner-up and don't want to seem upset, it will reflect badly on you.

thanking someone for an award

'Caitlin. It's Steve Harvey-Barham. I've just opened your letter informing me that I've won the society's annual award. I'm really pleased and flattered to be honoured in this way.'

'You deserve it, Steve. Your work was absolutely splendid. The judges were very impressed, especially with the Wilkinson family portrait – all those dogs and cats! Outstanding work.'

'Well, it's kind of you to say so. I was well trained, though, wasn't I? By Peter and Janice... I've always tried to produce something a little different and out of the ordinary, and this is a terrific recognition of that. It's a prestigious award...'

comments

1. If – or hopefully, when – you are notified that you are to receive an award of some kind, your response should be prompt, and a mixture of pleasure and modesty. This will convey the most favourable image, both of you and the company that you work for.

2. Open the conversation by saying how pleased you are to be honoured with this award, and perhaps adding that it is an unexpected surprise, or something similar. Talk modestly about your work, or whatever you were nominated for, as relevant, and praise those who have helped you – colleagues, and so on. Compliment the other person's organisation by speaking positively about the award. Then thank them again.

thanking someone for a present

'Meryl? It's Jim. Jim McRimmon. How are you?'

'I'm fine, Jim. And yourself?'

'Very well. I'm calling to thank everyone for the chess set you gave me as a leaving present. It's really unusual. Where did you find it?'

'I'm not sure, exactly. Karen got it from one of the antique shops on the North Road. Do you like it?'

'It's fantastic. I'm going to put it in the study on that table by the window overlooking the pear tree. It'll go nicely there. It's an excellent choice, Meryl – I couldn't have chosen better myself!'

'Oh, I'm so pleased you like it. We weren't sure if you would do as it's so unusual, but we thought it was a bit different – and better than the usual gift tokens we've been giving lately!'

'Yes, I'm really pleased with it. Thank you again, and please thank everyone else too.'

comments

1. The key to a successful telephone call of this nature is enthusiasm – it is as plain and as simple as that. Of course, this can be easier said than done, especially if you think the present is a hideous one!
2. Begin by thanking them for the present and talking a little about it – where you will put it, how you will use it, or whatever. Try to sound excited, even if you aren't. Compliment them on their choice – how they must have put so much thought into it, how well it suits you, and the like. Use plenty of positive words and expressions here. Conclude by thanking them again and wishing them well.
3. Ring solely to thank them for the present, rather than mention it during a conversation on another topic as this will lessen the effect. Alternatively, you may prefer to send a handwritten note of thanks, perhaps in a small card.

sympathising with someone on the loss of their job

'Hello, Arthur, it's Les Symonds at Haytons. I've just heard the news of your redundancy, and wanted to say how sorry I am about it.'

'Thanks... thanks, Les. It's a blow, I can tell you.'

'It must be. It seemed so unexpected, Arthur. What happened?'

'I don't really know. There had been some rumblings for a while now about exports and the problems we had with the Far East markets. But we never imagined there would be redundancies in this division, let alone so many. It's dreadful, Les, it really is...'

'I know. At least you've got a lot to offer another employer though, Arthur. So much experience. And all those courses you've been on must have kept you up-to-date on what's going on in the industry. You've got so much going for you. What are your plans?'

'Oh... I've no ideas at the moment to tell you the truth... it's not sunk in yet. I think I'm still in a state of shock!'

'Let me know if I can help, Arthur. You've always been good to me. We've nothing here, but I can probably put you in touch with some people who may be able to do something. Give me a call when you've decided what to do...'

comments

1. You may wish to make a call of this nature for two main reasons. On a personal level, you might like and respect the person, and sympathise with their situation. Perhaps they have helped you in the past. In business terms, such a call can enable you to discover useful information about their company and consolidate a good relationship with the person, which is particularly beneficial if subsequently they move to a position of power and influence.
2. Begin by expressing your regret and indicating that the news came as a complete surprise to you, if this seems appropriate. It can be sensible to state that it is the job that is being made redundant, not the person. This is especially worthwhile if the person sounds demoralised.
3. If you want to find out about what is happening at the firm, you could ask gently about the reasons behind the redundancy. Many people who have just lost their job are often willing to 'think out loud' and will share their thoughts with you at this time. Be careful here,

though, and make sure that you distinguish between facts and (highly emotional) opinions.

4. Do offer some encouragement during the conversation. Probably the best way to do this is to refer to the person's strengths and what they have to offer a new employer. Concentrate on those skills that are most transferable – computer literacy, keyboard skills and so on.
5. Ask about their plans for the future. It will obviously be helpful to know what they intend to do and where they would like to go, especially if it is somewhere they may be of benefit to you.
6. At some stage during the conversation, you may be asked if you know of any job vacancies or can help in any other way – typically, by circulating their details to your contacts in the trade or industry. If you make a call of this kind, you must expect a response of this nature and should be prepared to offer some form of assistance – for example by suggesting people who may be worth approaching. At the very least, you should be ready to say that you will bear them in mind in case you hear of any possible opportunities. Do so, and follow up your promise as appropriate.

sympathising with someone on a business failure

'Ken. It's Bryan Geddes. Rajesh has just told me that you're closing your business at the end of the year. I know we're in competition, but I'm sorry to see this happen.'

'Well... you know what it's like, don't you? Recession... tough competition from the multiples... it's too much. For us, anyway. You're lucky where you are, being that bit

further away from the superstore. We're too close. I'll tell you this in confidence, Bryan – our turnover's dropped 30 per cent since it's opened. You tell me how we can survive against that.'

'No one could, Ken. We certainly couldn't. I doubt anyone could, to tell you the truth. So what are your plans then, Ken?'

'We're keeping it going to the beginning of December and we'll then have the biggest pre-Christmas sale imaginable to clear as much as possible. We'll get what we can for what's left and the equipment, and then have the best possible Christmas that we can!'

'What will you do after that?'

'Goodness knows. Olivia will probably go to work at her father's timber merchants. She worked there before we got together. I'll probably use what money's left to set up as an agent. I know Elkie Broom is looking for someone in this area, and there are one or two other things floating about.'

'That sounds like a good idea. You'd be good at that, and you know as much as anyone about the trade, don't you? Have you thought about speaking to Sharon Talbot at ERS? I heard Stan English is winding down… might be worth a call.'

'Yes… yes, it might well be. Thank you, Bryan.'

'If you're looking for a buyer for your stock and equipment, let me know. I'd be interested. I'm sure we could sort something out that would be good for both of us. I'm sure I'd give you more than selling it to one of those market traders or bankrupt job lot merchants…'

comments

1. In many ways, this is a similar type of call to the preceding one on page 129, made to someone who is losing their job. Again, you may have personal feelings of sympathy for the owners and/or managers concerned, but you might also wish to benefit from the call – typically, by purchasing their equipment and stocks at a discount price or by having their customers redirected to your firm. Clearly, this call needs to be handled in a diplomatic manner.
2. Start by offering your sympathies and perhaps indicating that trading conditions are very difficult for everyone at the present time, if this seems appropriate. This gets them on your side. Talk to them on a personal level about what they have to offer and their plans for the future. Be prepared to offer some form of practical assistance (use of your computer, for example), especially if you are asked to do so. As in the example, introduce what you want from them towards the end of the call, saying how this will help both parties.

sympathising with someone on the death of their partner

'Hello, Alex. It's Christopher Piper.'

'... Chris... Hello, how are you?'

'I'm okay. I'm telephoning on behalf of all your friends here at the factory to say how sorry we all are to hear about Ashley.'

'Thanks... thank you. Yes... it is a great shock... being as sudden as that.'

'Is there anything any of us can do?'

'No, no, I don't think so. I can't think of anything. My sister's here anyway. She's doing it all. It was so sudden...'

'Yes, it was.'

'You know, I can't help thinking...'

comments

1. For most people, this is the hardest type of telephone call they will have to make; it is certainly the most difficult personal conversation you are likely to have with a well-established customer, supplier, employee, or whoever. Often, the less you say, the better – be led by the other person who may just want someone to talk to. There are various dos and don'ts to consider here.
2. Do avoid the (almost automatic) 'How are you?' greeting, which is insensitive, especially as the answer is obvious. Similarly, do not ask about or refer to the cause of death, particularly if it was sudden and/or unpleasant. It is often sensible to offer to provide some form of practical support, rather than intrude on too personal a level. Be guided by their response – for example whether they want to talk about their partner or not.
3. Be ready to praise their partner if this seems appropriate within the flow of the conversation, keeping your comments simple and focusing on the person's human qualities, rather than on their business skills. Don't use euphemisms and clichés such as 'fallen to sleep', 'a blessed relief', 'gone to a better place', 'time is a great healer', and the like. These sound clumsy and embarrassing and, again, are often insensitive. Accept that there is very little you can say – hopefully, just

being there and showing that you care is the best that can be done in such circumstances.

4. It is sensible to bear in mind that people in mourning often just want to be left alone immediately following a death and that phone calls – however well intended – may be seen as an unwanted intrusion. Therefore, this possibility is worth checking with someone who knows them extremely well before you make that call. It may be more sensitive simply to send a handwritten note or card to them instead, so that they know you are thinking of them and are there if needed.

6

managing miscellaneous calls

All sorts of calls will have to be managed by you while you are at work – to and from customers, suppliers and staff, and with a broad range of other people and organisations, too. Some will be particularly difficult, including:

- those involving requests for donations to charities;
- those made or received with regard to favours, promises and obligations that have not been kept;
- those concerning the media, either seeking publicity or trying to avoid it;
- various calls of an emotional nature – for example, to the emergency services.

asking for a donation

'… As I'm sure you know, Don Smith died last month and spent his last few weeks in the St Elizabeth hospice in Argyle Street.'

'Yes, I heard about Don. A sad business. Very sad indeed.'

'Well, we've been speaking to Don's widow, Mary, and the hospice, and have decided to set up a fund to help them to build a new sun lounge for the residents. It'll be a kind of practical memorial to Don. We've set ourselves a target of £12,000 to be raised by the spring.'

'And you're asking us for a donation?'

'If you're able to and would like to, then yes, please. The hospice really does need this. The love and attention given to the patients is absolutely first rate, but the premises are very cramped and limited. Also, because of the patients' condition and the weather, it's rarely possible for them to spend as much time out-of-doors as they would like. This sun lounge offers a solution.'

'What sort of sum did you have in mind?'

'Whatever you would like to give. Donations have ranged from £20 from one of Don's customers up to £500 from us. Everyone who makes a donation will be listed on a plaque that will be put in the sun lounge when it is opened by the mayor, hopefully next May or June.'

'All right, leave it to me. I'll have a word with Brendan and Diane, and see what we can do for you.'

'Thank you. We've produced a small brochure about this, along with a donation form. Shall I pop one in the post to you tonight, to give you something to look over and discuss with your partners?'

comments

1. Clearly, this is a tricky call to make. To be successful, you really need to know the person well, have a good cause that is close to their heart and be able to approach them in an appropriate manner. You have to be slightly detached from the subject rather than

emotionally involved, which would make it likely that you would overlook some key points and perhaps emphasise less relevant ones.

2. Begin by providing them with the basic facts – typically, who has set up the cause, why, and what it is aiming to achieve and by when, as relevant. Ask for a donation and explain what it would be spent on, and how this will benefit the recipient.
3. Those who are thinking of making a donation, and especially businesses, will often want to know what's in it for them – they might wish to see their name on a plaque, a list of contributors, or whatever. Some may be reluctant to admit to this, though, so it can be a good idea to refer to it at some stage in the conversation. Even if they respond by saying that this is not a consideration, it sometimes is.
4. If they are prepared to make a donation, you need to make it as easy as possible for them to do so. Ideally, you should be in a position to take credit card details over the phone. Alternatively, have various facts and figures at your fingertips – to whom cheques should be made payable, where they should be sent, paid in and so on. If they are not ready yet, you should try to encourage them to allow you to forward literature and other information to them to be studied later on. A follow-up call can then be made, if appropriate.

thanking someone for a donation

'Maureen? It's Jennifer Walton at Ampex. I'm just telephoning on behalf of the Marc Ridgely Appeal Fund to thank you for your firm's donation towards his "Wonderworld" fund. It was very kind of you. Thank you.'

'Oh, yes... hello, Jennifer. How is he?'

'He's fighting. He's still undergoing treatment at St Clements, but his Mum and Dad are cautiously optimistic. He's a real trooper; so, fingers crossed.'

'And the fund? Have you reached your target?'

'Not yet, no. We've just over £1,650 and are working towards the £2,000 we need to send Marc on holiday. We're doing our best to reach the target on time...'

comments

1. If a donation is made over the telephone in response to a request (see page 136), you would obviously thank that person immediately. If it is sent afterwards, perhaps as a result of studying literature, you should consequently call and thank them. This is polite and courteous, and makes it more likely that they will contribute again in the future. If donations have not yet reached their target on this occasion, your call may also encourage them to make a further contribution now.
2. As is often the case, the most effective call is the simplest one, so start by thanking them for their donation and saying what it has been used for. Almost inevitably, they will ask you how the fund-raising is progressing; if it has not yet reached its target, you can use this as an opportunity to say so and to encourage that additional contribution. Conclude by thanking them again, as appropriate, then put their details on your database for further communication as and when relevant.

the request for a donation, positive response

'That sounds like a worthy cause. Can you tell me what sort of amounts other firms and individuals have donated?'

'All donations are gratefully received. We've had schoolchildren sending us their pocket money. There's no ceiling on donations from larger concerns like yourself. Everyone has been very generous. Jacqui Reece at Analox gave £200.'

'Well, we have a smaller charitable budget here and it's almost fully committed at this time of year, but I think we can donate £100 on this occasion. Will there be a register of companies who have made donations?'

comments

1. Sometimes you will be asked to donate something to a good cause. This can be a difficult conversation to manage, even if your response is favourable. Typically, you may not know what is the 'right' amount to give, neither wishing to be over-generous, nor to appear mean. Also, you might wish to learn how your firm will benefit from such a donation – an understandable reaction from business people. Occasionally, you will find that you are being asked for more than you are willing to give, and this needs to be handled carefully.
2. If you wish to know what others have donated, the best way of doing this is simply to ask the caller about it; their response may enable you to conclude what is an appropriate amount to give on this occasion. Similarly, should you want to discover if and how your firm will gain from such a donation, ask if there will be a list of contributors – a plaque or whatever seems to be the most relevant in the situation.

3. Be aware that some charities will try to encourage you to donate more than you are willing to provide by employing a variety of tactics. Typically, the caller will suggest a minimum amount to be given (which seems quite high) rather than whatever you wish to give. Also, they may imply that other organisations similar to your own have been very generous, and they may perhaps quote one or two examples by name. Note that these may be the exception rather than the norm. Decide what you want and can afford to give, and donate this and no more – as in the example conversation below, you can state that you have a limited budget for charity.

the request for a donation, negative response

'… I wish we could make a contribution, Deborah; it is a good cause. Unfortunately, though, we're inundated with charitable requests, especially at this time of year, and the money that's been set aside for donations is fully used up. I'm sorry, but I do wish you well with your fund-raising.'

comments

1. Turning down a request for a donation is always a tricky task. Evidently, you do not want to run the risk of offending a prospective customer (or whoever is asking you for a contribution), nor to damage your firm's reputation in the community. Thus, it has to be done with great care and skill.
2. Probably the best way of handling such a call is to thank them for the request and to suggest that you receive innumerable approaches from similar worthy

causes (which may well be the case). Indicate that you would like to contribute to all of them if possible, but have a limited budget available for charitable purposes, and that this is fully committed at the present time. Decline politely and wish them success with their campaign.

asking for a favour

'Ben? It's Neil Gillespie at Head Office. Can you do me a favour?'

'Yes, I'm sure I can. What do you want me to do?'

'I really need to see a copy of the Cruikshank and Laing contract today. Can you go down and get the original for me, and fax it through to me? My fax number is 01903 674717...'

comments

1. Asking someone to do you a favour should be a relatively easy call to make if you know each other well enough to be able to make that request, and if they are willing and in a position to carry out the favour. This type of call is only difficult, and unlikely to succeed, if these criteria are not met.
2. Keep it simple – say that you are calling to ask a favour, outline what it is you want, make it easy for them to agree and do it by providing them with any information and/or materials they may need, and then thank them. Do not confuse or complicate matters by being circumspect or offering to do something in return. This can sound like a clumsy bribe – potentially offensive and unnecessary anyway if those key criteria are fulfilled.

the request for a favour, positive response

'Hello, Ruth. It's Roy Davey. I'm after a favour. Can you oblige?'

'If I'm in a position to do so – yes. Tell me what it is.'

'Well, I see from your call schedule that you're due to visit Queenie Gates at Goslings on Friday. Can you pick up a "Montmartre" for me? I promised to get one for my sister-in-law, and Queenie's the only person I know who has them in stock.'

'I'd be happy to help if I can. Does Queenie know about this?'

'No, not yet. I thought I'd check with you first.'

'Well, I'm happy to collect one as long as she knows about it. Can you give her a call now to tell her? Also, what about payment? Will you sort that out direct with her?'

'Yes, leave it to me. I'll ring her now and get it all sorted out.'

'Will you then call me back to confirm the arrangements, please?'

comments

1. There will be occasions when you are asked to do a favour for someone and may be happy to oblige if you are in a position to do so. However, you need to be careful that you do not establish a precedent that will lead to endless requests for help and assistance that you might not be able or want to agree to.
2. To minimise this possibility, your response to the request should be a qualified one, along the lines of

'yes, if I can'. Ask for further details before agreeing to it. Include some form of proviso to put a limit on what you are able to do, both now and in the future. Obtain supporting information and/or documentation, as in the example conversation.

the request for a favour, negative response

'Good afternoon, Archie. It's Edwin Kelliher. Can you do me a favour?'

'If I'm able to, I will. What is it?'

'I need someone to take over and finish the Risby deal. Can you do it?'

'I wish I could help you, Edwin, but I just don't have the time. I'm up to my neck in the Howlett and Palfrey projects, and am up against the deadlines. I can't take on anything else until next month at the earliest. Have you tried Pat Coggeshall?...'

comments

1. Turning down someone's request for a favour is always difficult, no matter what your reason – typically, because you do not know them that well, are unable to do whatever it is they want or are unwilling to do so due to your other commitments and obligations. Unfortunately, such a refusal can often cause offence and damage relations with that caller.
2. To avoid this requires a diplomatic response. Probably the best approach is to indicate that you would like to provide the help required but are not able to do so because of circumstances beyond your control –

company rules and regulations, the demands on your time, or whatever seems most appropriate in the situation. If you know someone else who may be able and willing to help on this occasion or feel that you might be in a position to in the future, say so now.

offering a favour

'Hi, Leslie. This is Aidan at Bowden Brothers. How are you?'

'I'm fine. And yourself?'

'I'm well. Look, I've just been talking to Lisa Riley and she mentioned that some shops were having problems getting hold of Gold Star's "Highlander De-luxe" models. Does that apply to you?'

'Yes, yes it does. They took our order at the trade fair in March and promised us delivery by the end of August. Then it was September. Then October. Now they're saying it'll be December. It's ridiculous.'

'Well, I don't know why, but we've had our delivery, and I'd be happy to let you have half-a-dozen, if it will help you.'

'... that's very good of you. Yes, it would help us out – enormously.'

'You've helped us in the past, particularly when we had that trouble with Caribo. And I know you'd do the same if the positions were reversed. So, do you want to come and collect them, or shall I drop them off?...'

comments

1. Telephoning someone to offer to do them a favour should be a relatively straightforward call if you know each other well, if you are able to help and they are

willing to accept your assistance without obligation. Unfortunately, problems can arise because the recipient of the call suspects that you have an ulterior motive, and/or does not wish to be in your debt.

2. Start by saying that you are aware that they have a problem or are experiencing difficulties in a particular area. Indicate that you may be in a position to help them and, if appropriate, that this would be without obligation. You may wish to refer to what they have done for you in the past, by way of explanation for your offer of assistance. Make your offer, inviting them to take you up on it should they wish to do so. Don't push too hard – the offer is there, but only if they wish to accept it.

the offer of a favour, positive response

'That's very kind of you, Suzanna. Thank you. I'd appreciate your help. Is there anything I can do for you?'

'No, not at the moment, but I'm sure there's something I'll think of some time.'

'Well, let me know if I can do something similar for you over the next few weeks. I'd be pleased to do a comparable favour for you...'

comments

1. The difficulty with being offered a favour and accepting it is that you may be obliged to return the favour at some stage in the future. You may be reluctant to be under such an obligation in case the other person wants more than you are able and willing to

give. If you accept the offer of a favour, you must be prepared to do something in return at a later date.

2. Do at least put a limit on what you will do in return by indicating in this conversation that you will be happy to help them out with a similar favour in the foreseeable future. This will show that you acknowledge that you are in their debt, but only to a certain extent, and no more.

the offer of a favour, negative response

'... Joe, I've heard you're having a problem with staff sickness and are short of admin' cover, what with everyone going down with this flu bug. I've a freelance here who'd be happy to come across to help you out for a while. Would you like me to get her to give you a call?'

'Oh, that's a very kind offer, Ray, and I appreciate you thinking of me. But we've got things under control at the moment, with all of us pulling together. Thank you, though.'

'Are you sure? I thought you were short of cover?'

'Well, we do have some people off sick, but the rest of us are all in and have got everything under control. I really appreciate this call, Ray, and I'll come back to you if the position changes. Thanks again...'

comments

1. Sometimes, you will be offered a favour by someone – an introduction to a person of influence, the loan of some equipment, or whatever – and will be happy to accept this. However, there will be times when you will

want to refuse, perhaps because you have the situation under control, or, as likely, do not wish to be under an obligation to this person. Turning down a genuine offer is tricky. If it is not handled well, it may cause offence and can damage your relationship with the person who is trying to help you.

2. You need to manage this conversation in a positive and enthusiastic manner. Probably the best response to their offer is to thank them warmly, explain briefly (and in very broad terms) why their kind offer does not need to be accepted (repeating this assurance if necessary), thank them again, and say that you will be in touch if the situation changes. This way, you should maintain their goodwill, and avoid being in their debt.

calling a newsdesk

'Morning, newsdesk.'

'Good morning. My name's Dennis Race. I run the "Gym and Trim" fitness centre in Argyle Street. Two of our trainees are receiving their NVQ awards here at 2.30 on Friday. Can you send someone along to cover the story?'

'Hold on a minute... yes, we can. Do you want to fax some details through and I'll then see if we can arrange for a photographer to come along?'

'Thank you. Let me have your name and fax number and I'll fax something to you in a few minutes. Can you give me the name of your photographer as well so we can have someone ready to meet them?'

'Of course, my name is...'

comments

1. If you are responsible for handling the media – typically, the local and trade press – your main aim will be to promote your company, goods and services at every opportunity. One way of achieving this is to supply the media regularly with news and information that will be of interest to their (and your) audience so that they will want to publish or broadcast it, as appropriate.
2. The newsdesk of a local paper will deal with events and activities that are occurring now, or very soon, and are of immediate or short-term interest to readers. And most will have regional correspondents covering the different areas. Find out who covers your area and make contact with them. Telephone only when your news matches these criteria – state who you are, what–when–where and why something is happening, and what you want the newsdesk to do to cover it.
3. Be ready to provide some key facts and figures in a handout, either faxed through to the newsroom, or given to the reporter (or photographer) who attends. This makes it easier for them to produce something and increases the chances of accurate information being published.
4. Never prepare an article or take photographs yourself for the local press as they are unlikely to be used, not least because you will be taking work away from someone else. At best, the article will be rewritten, often with some important facts omitted or altered. Concentrate instead on obtaining the names of whoever will be handling coverage so that you can greet them properly when you meet and build up your network of contacts for the future.

calling a features editor

'I think you'll find this feature will be of real interest to your readers – after all, they're mainly small business owners and managers, and these are the people who will be most affected and are most worried by the forthcoming legislation. Clearly, this feature will tell them exactly what's going to happen, the likely effects and how they can handle them.'

'And you can do this yourself, can you?'

'Yes, I can fax or e–mail an article through to you this afternoon, and get some transparencies biked over to you at the same time to support it. Obviously, I'll put my name and numbers in the "Useful Contacts" section so that those readers who want a survey done before the legislation is brought in can give me a call to arrange something. Leave everything to me.'

comments

1. Sometimes, whatever it is that you want to publicise about your firm, products or services will be more suited to a lengthier feature than a short news piece. Accordingly, you will wish to contact the features editor of the relevant newspaper or magazine. Knowing them personally will make this call easier to manage, as is often the case, and will improve your prospects of success.
2. As before, when calling a newsdesk (see page 148), you may find it helpful to put across the details on a who–what–when–where–why? basis prior to asking them to promote this information in a feature, perhaps in the next edition of the magazine.
3. Be prepared to work hard to persuade them to cover the story, especially if it does not fit in with what they

plan to publish in forthcoming issues. Often, your best approach in such circumstances is to stress how a feature of this nature will attract and be of interest to their readers. This should be your main focus.

4. As always, make it easy for the listener to do what you want them to do. Trade magazines are usually more receptive to externally submitted articles and (transparencies of) supporting photographs than local papers are, so an offer to supply these for the features editor to look at might be a wise move. Failing this, a list of facts and figures – to make their work easier and increase accuracy – should be provided.

the press interview

'"If in doubt, throw it out" has always been our company policy. Obviously, the risk is minimal, but any risk is one risk too many for us, especially when children are involved.'

comments

1. As with many calls, the key to a successful press interview is preparation. You need to be fully familiar with the subject matter and have the facts and figures at your fingertips. It will be advantageous if you know the interviewer well – what they are like, how they will approach the task, phrase questions, and so on. The more practice you can get beforehand, the better – perhaps colleagues can help you here.
2. You will find it useful to have three or four statements that you want to make during the conversation – short and snappy summaries of the company's viewpoint of the subject, which can be used as a ready-made headline or as quotes.

3. It is sensible to have thought through all the questions you might be asked, and considered your replies and their follow-up questions prior to the interview. Be aware of what you are going to say, but without setting down all your detailed responses in print – the interviewer will not keep to your script!
4. Remain calm under pressure. You have your short statements, which can be rephrased and repeated as necessary, and your lists of facts and figures to refer to, so you have no reason to feel pressurised. If you do not know the answer to a particular question, it is usually best to say so, state that you will find out and then return the call at the agreed time. Do not guess or try to make up company policy on the spot, as you will often live to regret this. Work from a position of strength, which requires a strong knowledge base.
5. On those occasions when it is important that your comments and views are reported accurately, it is advisable to follow the interview by submitting by fax or e-mail a sheet of relevant quotes, facts and figures to the journalist. If you are particularly concerned about the consequences of inaccurate reporting, it is also advisable to tape conversations of this kind.

the radio interview

'We have with us this morning, Cathy Ward, head of human resources at KPG Barlow. She's going to talk to us about getting your first job. Cathy, what do you look for in a job applicant?'

'We look for various qualities, Nigel. First of all, they should be well prepared – this means knowing about the company and the job, and the type of person we want.'

'And how should they find out this information?'

'It's a matter of initiative. For example, if they ask us for a company brochure and a job description that describes the position, we'll send these to them. If they read these and the job advertisement carefully, they should be able to work out what qualifications, skills and experience are required for that particular job.'

'What other qualities should first-time applicants have?'

'Enthusiasm and a genuine interest in the job are important too. As an example, Nigel...'

comments

1. In some respects, radio and press interviews are similar – you are helping them to produce interesting copy for the paper or a more varied programme on the radio, and they are enabling you to promote your business, goods and services. However, the main difference is that the radio interview is usually being transmitted live as you speak – easy to forget if you are doing it over the phone – so any hesitation, stumble or silence will be heard by the audience, and is not a good advertisement for you or your firm.
2. Go on air only if you know your subject extremely well and can answer any question that is likely to be raised promptly, correctly and clearly. You are unlikely to be told what will be asked – pressure of work rather than deliberate awkwardness – so you must be ready for anything and capable of ad-libbing comfortably.
3. Be led by the interviewer, who will almost invariably be on your side and keen to produce a professional and informative interview for their listeners. They're there to provide a good show, not to embarrass

you. Listen closely to their first question, answer it specifically, pause, let them ask the next one, and so on. Allow them to lead you through the conversation.

4. Keep your answers short and to the point – response, a brief explanation and an example, as appropriate. Remember that you are probably addressing a general audience, so use simple words and define other ones, as necessary. You may find it helpful to have a checklist of key words and phrases to refer to in case of hesitation, but be wary of becoming over-reliant on this.
5. Be careful not to repeat yourself – in particular, those key words and phrases. In a newspaper interview, it will be ignored. On the radio, it will irritate, again and again and again. If you stumble, it is usually best to pause and gather your thoughts before going on. Don't forget that the interviewer is there to assist you. Never try to bluff your way through with a joke ('Must get these teeth fixed!') as this just draws attention to the error. And, unless you are an experienced and skilled radio interviewee, it may be painfully unfunny.

declining an interview

'David? Is that David Harper?'

'Yes, speaking.'

'Hello, David, this is Nick Ash at SuperTrader. *We met at the Comp-Ex 2000 event last month. Look, we're running a feature in next month's issue about the products that are being launched in the autumn. Do you have a couple of minutes?'*

'No, I'm sorry, Nick. We're not releasing any information on them at the moment. I'll send you some details as soon as I can, but I can't help you now.'

'Are you sure? It would be good advance publicity for you.'

'No, I can't comment, Nick. I'm sorry.'

'Is there anyone else available I can talk to?'

'No, it's company policy not to provide any information at this stage. I can't add anything to that.'

'Okay, but I think you're missing a great opportunity here.'

'Thanks for calling, though, Nick. I'll be in touch. 'Bye.'

comments

1. Handling the media successfully involves more than promoting your company, goods and services at every opportunity. You also need to exercise as much control as possible over what is published and when. Also, it is important that a good working relationship is maintained with media representatives, so that future publicity is assured.
2. Be firm and decisive, saying 'no' straight away and giving a reason, while making it clear by your tone that this is not open to discussion. In the example, the recipient of this call starts no less than three sentences with that very emphatic word 'no'. Despite the caller's persistence, he does not waver at all.
3. You can discourage a discussion by making short and concise statements, and not responding to the caller's comments and questions. As shown in this example, the recipient does not react favourably to mentions of 'good advance publicity' and 'a great opportunity', effectively blocking the conversation.

4. Be friendly and polite. Using the caller's (first) name, apologising for being unable to assist them and thanking them for calling, can all help to ensure that you remain on amicable terms.
5. You can leave the way clear for future publicity by indicating that you will be able to assist them at a later date, as the person in the example manages to do.

correcting an inccurate story

'*Saskia Deacon.*'

'Hello, Saskia, my name's Geoff Wilby from Abacus Products. You ran a feature about us in last night's edition and it contained inaccuracies that need to be corrected. Our employees all work on a flexi-time basis, not a temporary one. Also, we import component parts from the Far East, not the Middle East.'

'*I see. Who interviewed you?*'

'One of your trainees, Darren Alderton. We do need a correction. We're about to start a recruitment drive and offering flexi-time is a big draw; temporary work isn't. We'd also prefer our customers and suppliers to know that we trade with the Far East, rather than the Middle East.'

'*Can you leave it with me? I'll see what I can do.*'

'We've prepared a correction that we'd like to have published in the same place in tonight's edition. I'm going to fax it through to you now. Can you check it over and come back to me with your agreement in the next half-hour?'

'*Let me have a look at it and I'll call you back.*'

'Thanks very much. I look forward to it.'

comments

1. Sometimes, journalists will mishear what you say or will misread their notes and publish incorrect information. You can reduce the likelihood of mistakes occurring by supplying a written list of the key facts and figures, although even then, errors will arise occasionally. Insist on having significant and/or potentially damaging inaccuracies corrected as soon and as prominently as possible. You may have to be very persistent in these circumstances, as few people are willing to be seen to admit mistakes.
2. After introducing yourself, identify the inaccuracies straight away and correct them. Then state what you want and explain why, focusing on why the errors are detrimental to your firm. Stress the likely consequences, if necessary. Conclude by making it easier for them to help you – typically, by faxing through a copy of what you want to be included in a correction. Be ready to follow this through if you have to, making a chasing call or sending another e-mail or fax, as and when appropriate.

congratulating someone on a favourable story

'Taylor–Williams.'

'Hi, Dan. It's Jason Brown at Hamiltons. I just wanted to give you a quick call to say thanks for the feature in this month's *Gazette*. It was excellent publicity for us. Thank you.'

'Always happy to be of service.'

'Well we're really grateful. While I'm on, we're upgrading some of our products in the spring. Can I send you some details next month?'

'Sure, I'd be pleased to take a look at them.'

'Leave it with me, Dan. Thanks again for the feature. I'll speak to you soon.'

comments

1. To sustain a sound relationship with journalists and other people in the media, it is a good idea to acknowledge their help and thank them for it, as and when appropriate. A brief phone call is often sufficient, and can also create an opportunity for further contact and additional publicity in the near future.
2. Begin by explaining why you are calling and thanking them. This simply means saying 'thank you' – no more and no less than that. This basic but powerful phrase will often have a much greater impact than effusive comments, which can make you sound insincere.
3. Should you wish to follow this in order to boost your chances of forthcoming publicity, you can mention future activities to see how interested they are, consequently pursuing this as appropriate. Be cautious, though, as such comments can lessen the effect of that 'thank you', since they indicate that you called with an ulterior motive. Much depends on how well you know the person and whether or not further contact benefits both parties, or just you.

reminding someone of a promise

'... so I'd expect to hear from them some time next week, or the week after at the latest. By the way, Ron, have you had a chance to circulate my photos to your contacts yet?'

'Um, er... no, not yet. I've been really tied up with a couple of projects that had to be completed this month.'

'Would you like me to have some more photographs biked over to you this afternoon?'

'No, no... I've still got them somewhere. Leave it with me.'

'I really need to speak to these people this month, Ron. Can you let them have the photos this week?'

'Yes, I'm sure I can do that for you.'

'That's excellent, thank you. Will you let me know if you need any more photographs? I have some here. Thanks again, Ron.'

comments

1. Occasionally, a person will promise to do something that is important to you, but does not then carry it out. You then decide to contact them to find out why and, hopefully, to encourage them to take immediate action. This is a hard call to make, and is even more difficult if they promised to do you a favour. You will need to be at your most diplomatic if you are to ensure that promise is fulfilled and your working relationship with that person is to be maintained.
2. Because of the possible delicacy of the situation, it is often best to include this reminder (almost in passing) within another conversation, as indicated in the example. Avoid using the emotive word 'promise' or suggesting that they have let you down in any way by sounding angry or disappointed. It is sensible to accept and sympathise with whatever reason they give, subsequently concentrating on making it as easy as possible for them to fulfil their original promise. Try to get them to repeat that promise and state a deadline for completing it. Don't forget to thank them again, as and when appropriate.

reminding someone of an obligation

'Miss Buckland, when we spoke on the telephone at the end of last month, I agreed to accept your unsold goods back for credit to your account on the understanding that they were received by the middle of February. This was so that we could resell them before the close of the season. You agreed to do this, but we haven't received them. Can you tell me what's happening?'

'Ah, well now... We've had problems getting them packed up as we don't have the original boxes, you see. We're waiting for some big ones to come in and then we'll get what's left back to you straight away.'

'Yes, I can understand that may have been a problem, but we do need to sort this out now as time is running out. Do you still want to return these goods to us?

'Yes, I do. I'll sort it out.'

'Okay, but I do need to make our position clear to you. If the goods are received here by Friday, we will credit them to your account. We cannot accept them after that date, though, as we'll not be able to sell them on. So, if we haven't had them by then, the account will be passed to our debt recovery unit to be pursued in the normal manner...'

comments

1. Although this call appears to be similar to the preceding one on page 158, this one is made to a person who has failed to honour an obligation to you – for example, to pay an instalment on an agreed repayment schedule. They are indebted to you, rather than vice versa, which enables you to adopt a firmer,

more demanding stance, according to the circumstances.

2. In general, you should begin by referring to the obligation, stating that it has not been fulfilled and asking them for the reason(s). Listen and sympathise, as appropriate. You may wish to come to a revised agreement if relevant, perhaps rescheduling to take account of changed circumstances. Then ask them to honour the obligation, specifying a time limit for doing this, and stating what will happen if they do not. Be prepared to follow through, if you have to.
3. Clearly, the approach that you adopt will depend on many factors, not least how significant the obligation is, how long they have overlooked it, what their current circumstances are, and what the ongoing effects of not fulfilling it will be. If monies are owed, it is usually wise to strike a fair but very firm stance, to discourage other people from adopting a similar line.

inviting someone to an event

'Let me tell you who's speaking at the seminar. We've got Anthony Reynolds, Head of Business Information and Technology at Needale University. Now, I know your business has just set up a new Web site, so if you've any questions about the Internet and how small firms can benefit from it, Anthony's the person to ask. We've also got Sara Rowbeck, a management consultant and author of *Network Marketing*. I understand this is a growth area for you, so...'

comments

1. Before this call, it is sensible to think particularly hard about why the recipient would want to speak at a

conference, take an exhibition stand, attend a seminar, or whatever. To persuade someone to come, you will need to stress those benefits that will enable them to fulfil their goals. Perhaps have a note of these goals and the benefits of attendance close at hand when you make the call. Remember, tell them what's in it for them!

2. To start the conversation, enquire whether they are interested in coming to the event and, if so, provide brief details – the nature of the event, its purpose and activities, the likely participants, dates and location, as relevant. Giving them this information provides them with an opportunity to decline diplomatically should they wish to do so – typically, by claiming a prior arrangement at that time.
3. Next, say what you want from them – a 30-minute speech on a specified subject, the hire of stand space at a certain price, the purchase of a ticket to attend the event, and so on. It is sensible to state clearly at an early stage what their commitment would be – along with any other significant obligations – rather than try to gloss over them. This would only lead to further questions and concerns later on.
4. Specify what is in it for them, stressing how the benefits of coming will help them to meet their goals. As an example, you might concentrate on discussing the expected numbers and types of visitor to an exhibition if these are the kind of people whom the recipient wants to meet and, hopefully, to do business with.
5. Be prepared to answer clearly and directly any questions they may have about the event, and most notably what would be expected of them if they decide to attend. Too often, possible problem areas are not addressed until a later (contractual) stage, which can result in ill feeling and even withdrawals in some instances. When answering queries, remind the other

person of the benefits of coming to the event, as and when you can.

6. Conclude this conversation by making it easy for the person to accept your invitation, perhaps by stating that you can take a booking over the phone, will send details and a reservation form after the call, and so on. And follow through by faxing or posting that material immediately.

the invitation to an event, positive response

'... I'm interested in principle, although I'll need to check the dates with my diary and the company schedule before I can make a definite commitment. Before that, can you tell me how you think I will benefit from attending this event?'

comments

1. On occasions, you will be invited to an event – a conference, exhibition or whatever – and will be interested in attending in some capacity. Your initial response will be positive, but should be a qualified one, as you need to know all about the event before you make a final decision. Much of this information can be obtained during this conversation.
2. To begin with, ask for some basic facts and figures – for example, the nature of the event, its aims and content, who will be involved and attending, and its dates, times and location. These can be noted and used as a cause of rejecting the invitation if necessary (see page 164).
3. Next, discover what you are expected to do and/or pay for, as appropriate. Check the main terms and

conditions of agreeing to become involved with the event. It cannot be stressed enough that you need to find out as much as you can now, rather than later when it will be more difficult for you to withdraw amicably. Ask questions and request answers to them. Do not allow yourself to be fobbed off with platitudes and generalised assurances.

4. If the caller is vague or uncertain about anything – the names of the speakers, the location of the remaining exhibition stands available, and so on – ask them to obtain these details and come back to you to continue the conversation. You need this information now, before making your decision.
5. Consider in particular how speaking at this conference, exhibiting at this event, or whatever, will be of benefit to you. Think over your aims – to raise your personal profile in the industry, to make face-to-face contact with prospective customers, or whatever. Contemplate how far your participation in this event will help you to achieve them. If you feel that the benefits will be significant, you may wish to proceed, requesting written confirmation, a booking form, and so on. Otherwise, you should decline involvement (see below).

the invitation to an event, negative response

'… It sounds really exciting, Ravi, and I'm sure it will be a huge success for you, but I just can't make it. I've checked my diary for that week and it's full, and I'm not able to rearrange anything. I'm really disappointed. Could you let me know how it goes? Perhaps I can give you a call afterwards and you can bring me up-to-date on what happened…'

comments

1. Sometimes, you will be invited to participate in or attend events that you do not need or want to become involved with. There are no benefits there for you. If the invitation is made by telephone, it can be difficult to say 'no', especially if the caller is someone you like and/or wish to remain on amicable terms with.
2. Probably the best response to a verbal invitation is to thank them and express interest in the event. Then make a diplomatic excuse – meetings have been arranged at that time, you are short staffed, have prior commitments, or whatever. Express regret and ask to be told about what happens. You could even make a follow-up phone call after the event to obtain up-to-date news and information that might be of interest to you.

calling the emergency services

'Emergency. Which service?'

'Ambulance, please... My name is Ed Phelps. I'm phoning from Houghton 232300. I'm in the reception of Garnham and Moore, the motor dealers at the junction of London Road and Barrow Road in Houghton, West Sussex. We have a customer who has collapsed with a suspected heart attack. Please send an ambulance here immediately...'

comments

1. It is surprising how many people do not know how to handle a call to the emergency services in a swift and efficient manner. Consequently, they waste precious

time when they telephone for help in a crisis. The standard procedure is very simple.

2. After hearing the operator's question, state the service needed – typically, fire, police or ambulance (although the coastguard, mountain or cave rescue services may be required on occasions). Be prepared to give the number of the telephone you are calling from, if requested. Do not panic if you do not know and cannot see what it is – 999 calls can be traced immediately to the telephone where they are coming from.
3. The operator will then connect you to the appropriate service, and you should explain as briefly and as calmly as possible what the trouble is, where it is and where you are telephoning from. Be ready to repeat the details, spelling out names of roads and specifying their locations if necessary; bear in mind that emergency calls are rarely dealt with locally so some explanation of the location will often be required. The appropriate service will then be provided as soon as possible.

the obscene telephone call

'Felbury 4354.'

'...'

'Hello? Felbury 4354.'

'... *What are you wearing?*'

'I'm sorry?'

'Are you wearing anything?'

'.........................'

comments

1. If you receive an obscene call, the most sensible piece of advice that can be given – and it is often easier said than done – is to stay calm and in control. An emotional response is likely to excite the caller and encourage them further. Always remember that this is your telephone, so stay in charge.
2. Do not respond or enter into any conversation. Put the phone down alongside the handset and walk away. Resist the growing temptation to pick it up again and reply. After a few minutes, replace the telephone on the handset. If another call is made soon after or repeatedly, do not say anything as you lift up the telephone. A genuine caller will then speak first. Repeat the process again, as necessary.
3. Dialling 1471 will give you the number of the person who has just called you (unless they dialled 141 before telephoning). Obscene phone callers do not always remember to do this, so do try 1471. Also, you can contact British Telecom or your telephone service provider for further advice and assistance (see page 168).

the silent telephone call

'Tinbridge 64512.'

'......................'

comments

1. Silent phone calls can be as frightening as obscene ones, perhaps because the motive is less obvious and therefore more sinister. A silent call should be treated

in exactly the same way as an obscene one. Do not try to persuade the caller to speak – they want to hear you do this and to listen to you becoming angrier and more upset in the process. Just walk away from the telephone, and replace the receiver later on.

2. Always obtain help from British Telecom, or your telephone service provider, on any malicious calls. BT has a free advice line for information on how to handle unwanted calls and what they can do to assist you. Phone 0800 666 700. Alternatively, telephone their Specialist Bureau free of charge on 0800 661 441. Specially trained investigators will work with you to resolve the problem. They can also work with the police to trace these calls. This is a criminal offence and such callers can be and are prosecuted.